SISSY GOFF & DAVID THOMA

MW00697981

Raising
Boys
& Girls

The Art of Understanding Their Differences

ISBN: 1415869936
Item Number: 005371583

Dewey Decimal classification Number: 649
Subject Heading: BOYS / GIRLS / CHILD-ADULT RELATIONSHIP

Printed in the United States of America

Student Ministry Publishing
LifeWay Church Resources
One LifeWay Plaza
Nashville, Tennessee 37234-0174

We believe the Bible has God for its author; salvation for its end; and
truth, without any mixture of error, for its matter and that all Scripture is
totally true and trustworthy. The 2000 statement of The Baptist Faith and
Message is our doctrinal guideline.

TABLE OF CONTENTS

MEET THE AUTHORS
SISSY GOFF

Sissy Goff, M.Ed., LPC-MHSP, spends most of her days talking with girls and their families, with the help of her counseling assistant/pet therapist, Lucy the Havanese. She received her Master's in Counseling from Vanderbilt University and since 1993 has worked as the Director of Child and Adolescent Counseling at Daystar Counseling Ministries in Nashville, Tennessee. She is also the author of five books, including *Raising Girls, Modern Parents, Vintage Values, The Back Door to Your Teen's Heart*, as well as *Mirrors and Maps* (for 11-14-year-old girls) and *Growing Up Without Getting Lost* (for 15-19-year-old girls). Over the years, Sissy has spoken to thousands of parents and girls across the country, both at live events and on radio and television programs such as "Moody Mid-Day Connection," "FamilyLife Today," and "Faith and Family." She is also a frequent contributor to *ParentLife* magazine and *Living with Teenagers*.

MEET THE AUTHORS
DAVID THOMAS

DAVID THOMAS, L.M.S.W., is the Director of Counseling for Men and Boys at Daystar Counseling in Nashville, Tennessee. He is the co-author of five books, including the best-selling *Wild Things: The Art of Nurturing Boys* (Tyndale House Publishers). David is a frequent guest on ABC Family Channel's "Living the Life," "FamilyLife Today," "Moody Mid-day Connection" and "On the Home Stretch." He has written for numerous publications and speaks across the country on "Nurturing Boys, Parenting Adolescents, and Raising Kids of Character."

He did his undergraduate and graduate training at the University of Tennessee. He and his wife, Connie, have three children and a feisty yellow lab puppy named Owen.

MEET THE AUTHORS
MELISSA TREVATHAN

Melissa Trevathan, M.R.E., first became a youth director at the age of 16. Since that time, she has been a teacher, retreat leader, head of spiritual life at a private school in Nashville, and is now founder and Executive Director of a counseling ministry called Daystar Counseling Ministries that began in 1985. She is the author of five books including: *Raising Girls, Modern Parents, Vintage Values,* and *The Back Door to Your Teen's Heart,* as well as *Mirrors and Maps* (for 11-14-year-old girls) and *Growing Up Without Getting Lost* (for 15-19-year-old girls). Melissa has spoken to various churches and schools across the country, has taught graduate courses in counseling adolescents, and has been a guest on television and radio programs throughout the United States and Canada. She is a regular speaker at LifeWay's "You and Your Girl" events as well as a popular speaker for parents and kids of all ages. Melissa and her Old English sheepdog, Blueberry, divide their time between Nashville and Kentucky Lake.

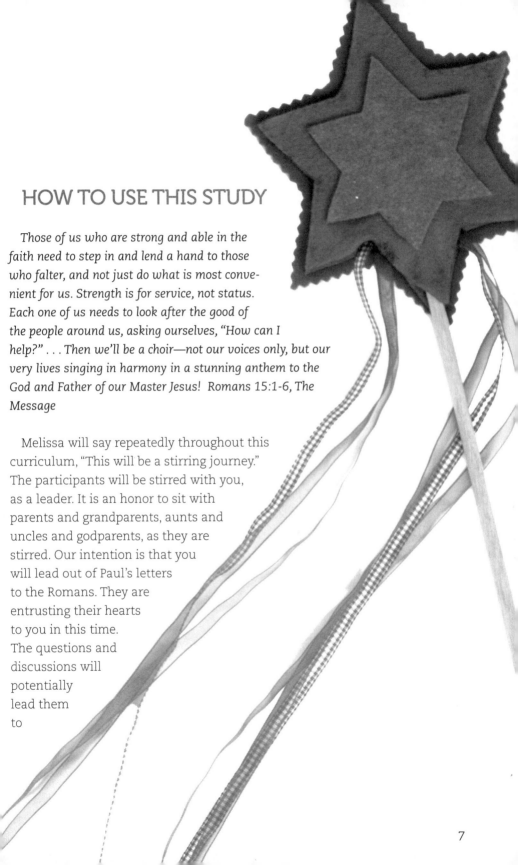

HOW TO USE THIS STUDY

Those of us who are strong and able in the faith need to step in and lend a hand to those who falter, and not just do what is most convenient for us. Strength is for service, not status. Each one of us needs to look after the good of the people around us, asking ourselves, "How can I help?" . . . Then we'll be a choir—not our voices only, but our very lives singing in harmony in a stunning anthem to the God and Father of our Master Jesus! Romans 15:1-6, The Message

Melissa will say repeatedly throughout this curriculum, "This will be a stirring journey." The participants will be stirred with you, as a leader. It is an honor to sit with parents and grandparents, aunts and uncles and godparents, as they are stirred. Our intention is that you will lead out of Paul's letters to the Romans. They are entrusting their hearts to you in this time. The questions and discussions will potentially lead them to deep, painful places. We hope that you will walk alongside them, rather than in front. They need you to be steady, to be constant and warm, in the way that Jesus is for us. We appreciate your willingness to take this journey with them—and us. We are praying for God's guidance and discernment for you and that they will be filled with hope—for themselves, as parents, and for the children they love.

For these groups to work, it is important that all of the participants agree to three items.

1 They need to keep confidentiality with the other participants. As we say in our groups at Daystar, what's said in this room stays in this room.

2 Everyone participates. It only works if each person is invested.

3 Honesty is key. We are going to ask questions that will require an honest look at themselves and honest answers.

They will receive as much from this as they are willing to invest. It might even help to have these words on a whiteboard each time they come into the room.

You will find different sections in this book that serve different purposes. The sidebars give suggestions to you as a leader: icebreakers, information to share, discussion questions to follow the video. Typically, each session would start with an icebreaker or introduction to the topic. Next, you would want to play the video that corresponds to that session. Each session in this book begins with a fill-in-the-blank listening guide that participants can complete as they listen to the video. Each guide is a basic outline of the content, but there is plenty of room for additional notes. You will then find a summary of the content, a section that relates where your child is to where you are as a parent, and suggestions for relating to both daughters and sons. This is material that can be reviewed during the week. Also, "Daily Conversations" are provided so that participants can have a short dose of encouragement each day of the week. Enjoy!

STIRRED TO LOVE

Stir—to set up a great unrest, to fire up, or to cause a slight movement.

Parenting is a stirring journey. From the very first moment your child enters your world, your heart will alternate between states of great unrest, slight movement, and being all fired up. You will be stirred. That is a promise. And you will be stirred even as you watch and read through the pages of this book. You may be stirred to fear, to frustration, to sadness, or to joy. But our hope, through it all, is that you will be stirred to love this child that has been entrusted to you.

Listening Guide

Icebreaker—
Direct each
parent to say
three words
that they
would use to
describe their
children.

For young men, the risk of looking like a ___fool___,

the fear of being embarrassed, is so much stronger than the

willingness to take the ___risk___ to just be who God has

___created___ them to be.

The girls were wondering, "Will I be left out? Will I just

be left standing here?" Underneath, they just want to be

___accepted___, to be ___enjoyed___, to feel

___safe___.

Underneath, the boys just want to have courage and

___strengh___. They want to be somebody. They just want

to have some kind of ___purpose___.

Madeleine L'Engle said that we are every ___age___ we have

ever ___been___.

One dad said, "I wish I'd known how much _impact_ I had."

Failure is _inevitable_. But the important thing is that you stay _connected_.

You may recognize a _stage_ you feel stuck in.

Our desire is that you will be stirred to _love_.

We pray that you remember that God has _chosen_ you to be the parent of your child.

We want you to be convinced that God is able to _protect_ what you have _entrusted_ to Him.

Summary

Do you have your own memories of middle school dances? The awkwardness and the creative tactics to cover up the awkwardness . . . giggles, sarcasm, communal trips to the bathroom, throwing ice? And do you remember how fearful you were underneath all of that awkwardness? Take a minute to picture yourself there.

You wanted to be chosen. You wanted purpose. To connect. To avoid looking like a fool. You wanted all of the things you were fearful you weren't. And the fear of not being those things was stronger than the desire to take a risk and be yourself.

Lead the participants to answer these questions:

How are you being stirred right now in your parenting?

When was the most recent time you felt a strong emotional response?

Parenting is really not that different. You want purpose . . . to connect . . . to feel chosen . . . to look like you have some semblance of an idea of what you're doing. But, more often than not, you don't. You're raising your child when you're not entirely sure you're finished being raised yourself. But here you are—as a parent—wanting to parent with all of the positives and none of the negatives that were a part of your own growing up. It is a stirring journey. It stirs up every emotion and fear that were a part of those awkward adolescent moments. And your fear of what you're not as a parent can often prevent you from being who you can be.

That's where we hope this curriculum will help. God has chosen you. Before you were born, He knew the way your son would ask you a million questions, believing you truly knew the answers. He knew the way your daughter would take your hand and trust you to lead her anywhere. He knew your teenage son's eye-rolling habit before your son's eyes opened for the first time. And he knew the knot you would have in your throat the day you walked your daughter down the aisle.

God has chosen you. You have, by His grace, all that you need to raise your son or your daughter. As you are stirred, through their lives and through this study, remember Hebrews 10:24.

May you be stirred to love. In the midst of all of the other stirrings, the stir to love can be strongest. It can be strongest because you have been chosen, and because the God who chose you is able to keep that which you have entrusted until the day you see Him face-to-face (2 Timothy 1:12).

■ How did you cope with middle school dances? What were they like for you? _____

_____

_____

_____

■ Do you see any similarities between the feelings then and the feelings you have today as a parent? _____

_____

_____

_____

_____

■ How do you escape now? _____

_____

_____

_____

■ Madeleine L'Engle said, "I am still every age that I have been."[1] What age do you feel that you are now? Why? _____

_____

_____

_____

Lead the participants to reflect on their own middle school dance experience and answer the following:

What were you wearing?

What music do you remember?

How did you feel?

■ Which of the three degrees of stirred do you feel as this study begins: a slight movement, great unrest, or fired up? What area is stirring you the most? _____

_____

_____

_____

_____

■ How would your parenting be different today if you were to believe that God had specifically chosen you to be your child's parent? _____

_____

_____

_____

_____

■ How would your parenting be different today if you believed that love can be stronger than all of the other feelings being stirred in you? _____

_____

_____

_____

_____

■ How would your parenting be different today if you believed that God is able to protect that which you have entrusted to him? _____

_____

_____

_____

_____

Parent Perspective

"I'm afraid to have a little girl. I don't want to be the kind of mom to her that my mom was to me."

"I was terrified when my son was born. I knew that to raise a man I had to know how to be one—and I still didn't have it figured out."

"I loved playing with my kids when they were younger. But once they became teenagers, I didn't know how to play with them anymore. I didn't really even know how to talk to them. I remember how uncomfortable I was with myself when I was their age, and I think I became equally uncomfortable with them."

As Madeleine L'Engle said, you are every age you've ever been. You parent out of who you are today, but also who you have been through all of your growing up. Your past is just as much a part of your parenting as is your present. And both will be stirred.

We've already talked about the present stirring. Your son is bullied at school, and everything inside of you wants to do a little bullying yourself. Your daughter is the only one of her friends who isn't asked to prom and you hurt just as much as she does. As a parent, you will feel the heights of joy and depths of sorrow that your son or daughter goes through on a daily basis.

But then there will be other times. There will be times that maybe you feel a little more sorrow than your son does over a dropped pass on the football field or a little more desperation that your daughter be a part of a certain group. A mom who brought her daughter to Daystar talked about how sad she was to watch her daughter after school. "She doesn't talk to anyone. The other girls are laughing, walking arm in arm, making plans. She keeps her head down and walks straight to the car." It was clear that this mom was very outgoing. She spent her

Lead the participants each to talk about the environment of their home growing up . . .

Who lived there?

What were three words to describe each person's personality?

Pick a television show—past or present— that your family most resembled.

Teaching Tip: You may notice that you have one group member who talks more than the others. It can help to divide the time into equal segments, telling them how long they each have to answer questions.

growing up years with friendships being her highest priority. Her daughter, however, sees things a little differently. "I have good friends I sit with at lunch and play with at recess. But, when school is over, I'm ready to go home. I just want to be in my room by myself." The daughter is obviously more introverted than her mom. She doesn't have the same need to connect that her mom had when she was her age.

So, what is happening in this case? Her mom is parenting out of her adult self, as well as her third-grade self. It's a bit like the Disney movie, *The Kid*. (If you haven't seen it, we would suggest you watch it . . . it's a family-friendly film, too, by the way.) If you've seen it, you know that Bruce Willis's character as an adult is still haunted by the chubby boy he was when he was growing up. He lives with all of the same insecurities, hopes and fears. You will, too, as a parent. And you will be stirred on both levels—as a parent and as the 8-, 11-, or 15-year-old inside of you.

You are every age you've ever been. Andy Stanley says, "It is when our hearts are stirred that we are most aware of what they contain." Your heart contains a lifetime of memories and feelings. You can't separate those memories and feelings out of who you are, just because you become a parent.

Every time we teach a parenting class and talk about development, at least one parent comes up to talk about himself or herself. The comments range from "I think maybe I got stuck somewhere along the way" to "I couldn't help but think about how I never got that when I was growing up." These parents are listening with their 12- and 20-something-year-old selves. They are being stirred on both levels. As counselors, we love it when this happens. We love it because the hearts of these parents are coming to life in a way that can help them connect more deeply with themselves, their children, and with God.

So, what do we want you to do with these stirrings . . . stirrings from the present and the past? We want you to listen. We want you to pay attention, to follow them to see where they lead. This section of the study, for each chapter, will give you an opportunity to dig a little deeper into your story. Your story, past and present, is a part of why God has chosen you to raise your son or daughter.

"To cleave the truth of our own lives, to lift and look beneath our own stones, is to see glimmers at least of his life, of his life struggling to come alive in our lives, his story whispering like a song through the babble and drone of ours." –Frederick Buechner

~TRY IT OUT~
For Parents of Girls

" 'It's a girl,' the ultrasound nurse declared as she guided the gel-coated device across my belly. My heart skipped a beat. My firstborn had been a son, nearly two years before. So far, my only perception of my parenting self was as a boy-mom. I made boys. That's what I did.

This news of a daughter filled me with so much emotion that I couldn't let myself open up to it until I was outside the clinic, standing alone in the parking lot. Then my mind and my heart started to expand, and an unfamiliar and unexpected wave of wonder and relief and gratitude came rushing up from deep inside. I was carrying a baby girl who would one day become a woman. And that woman, if loved and respected, might someday become a friend with whom I could share the rest of my days." –Amy Grant

These words are the beginning of Amy's gracious introduction to our book, *Raising Girls*. We would guess that, at some point, you had a similar experience. Maybe it was at your ultrasound when you found out you were having a little girl. Maybe it was when you chose her name. Or maybe even the instant she was born. Your heart flooded with emotion and your imagination flooded with images. What would it be like to have a little girl? What did you picture in those moments?

A friend of ours who just had his first daughter after two sons said, "It's amazing how different it was from the moment I held her. She seemed so fragile. Something rose up in me that wanted to protect her."

What rose up in you? What did the idea of a daughter stir up in you then and what does the reality of a daughter, whatever her age, stir in you now? How is what you imagined different and similar to what life is like with a little girl?

The rest of our "try it out" sections in the book will give you suggestions as to how to connect with your daughter at each stage of her development. But, for now, we want you to continue in this rhythm of stirring and listening. Your daughter has, from the first moment you knew about her, stirred you in ways that no one else ever will. What are those ways? And what do they say about you, about her, and about a God who has chosen you both to journey together?

~TRY IT OUT~
For Parents of Boys

I can still remember what I was wearing the day of our second ultrasound—jeans and a plaid button-up.

I can still remember where I was sitting when the words were spoken. Actually, I was standing when we got the news, and I immediately had to sit down. I must have gone pale, because the ultrasound technician stopped attending to my wife and began asking if I needed anything.

I had been a father for a little over a year to this delicate, gentle-natured, fair-skinned little blonde who was the spitting image of my wife. I was just beginning to wrap my mind around the unique blessing of parenting a little girl, when the technician announced that my wife was carrying twins . . . and both had the anatomy identifying them as boys.

I am still recovering from that news 10 years later.

My family, friends, and colleagues found it strange that my initial response to the news of sons involved more fear than joy. They all know me as someone who loves boys. My practice as a therapist involves working primarily with boys, adolescent males, and young men. I've been teaching classes for years on nurturing boys. My world is boys, boys, and more boys. So why the fear?

The fear comes from living in this world of boys. After seeing hundreds of them over the last decade of my practice, I know how they think, what makes them tick, and all the confusing, impulsive, complicated things they say and do. Furthermore, every year I interact with hundreds of parents who are confused and bewildered by the journey of raising sons. That day in the OB-GYN's office, I knew just enough to be frightened (actually terrified) by the news that my wife was carrying two of these strange creatures in her womb.

Equally, I feel this weighty responsibility to help contribute a few decent men to the world. My wife once commented about how many great women she'd had the opportunity to know, to work alongside, and to journey with in friendship, and that she could count the really exceptional men she knew on two hands. (Many women in this world could count the number of exceptional men they know on one hand.) I think there's a reason Flannery O'Connor titled her most famous work *A Good Man is Hard to Find*.

I hope the conversations we'll have throughout the "Try It Out's" will be a time to explore parenting these fascinating, confusing, imaginative, complicated, energetic, impulsive, sensitive, action-oriented creatures we know as boys. We'll keep studying who they are and paying attention to what they need. We'll experiment with a number of different ideas throughout this section as we try and get access to their hearts and minds. We'll journey together in the privilege we've been given to participate in contributing a few good men to this world.

Daily Conversations

Stop and Look

"Moses was shepherding the flock of Jethro, his father-in-law, the priest of Midian. He led the flock to the west end of the wilderness and came to the mountain of God, Horeb. The angel of God appeared to him in flames of fire blazing out of the middle of a bush. He looked. The bush was blazing away but it didn't burn up. Moses said, 'What's going on here? I can't believe this! Amazing! Why doesn't the bush burn up?' God saw that he had stopped to look. God called to him from out of the bush, 'Moses! Moses!'" –Exodus 3:1-4, *The Message*

Moses looked. The angel of God appeared to him, and the text makes it a point to say those two words: *He looked.* We could say that he was stirred. He probably felt a lot when he saw the angel in the bush . . . fear, curiosity, wonder. But in the midst of those feelings, Moses stopped, turned away from his flock and took the time to look. And then "God saw that he had stopped to look." God met Moses near the burning bush when he stopped.

All of this stirring we're talking about can be a difficult thing. You have homework to help with and soccer games to watch. Work takes up most of your time. It's easier just to ignore the stirrings. Keep plodding through your day. Maybe there will be time to look later.

But the bush still burns. You still feel something flicker inside your chest as you watch your husband delight in your daughter when your dad never seemed to notice you. You feel intense pressure that your son make straight A's so that he has all of the opportunities you didn't.

Stop. Look. Pay attention to the stirring. When Moses stopped to look, God was right there in front of him. He is with us, too.

What do you notice this day as you stop and look? Take a minute to write about what God might want to say to you.

Acting and Reacting

Last night, I (Melissa) ran into a father who was quite stirred. I was parking my car at the movie theater when my dog, Blueberry, started growling. Before I saw the father, I heard him. Blueberry must have, too. He was standing beside his car, yelling loudly at his teenage son. The son just stared. "You're nothing but a lazy _____. You never listen to a thing I say." He yelled for a few more minutes when the son turned, and walked away without a word. The father yelled louder. "Get your _____ back here! I'm talking to you." There is no telling what stirred this father, but something did. And the father reacted. He reacted to something his son had done and followed him, getting more and more angry with every step.

Let's go back to Moses. If we go a little further in the story in Exodus, Moses did some reacting of his own. God told Moses that he wanted him to go and speak to the Israelites. Moses' stirring turned to fear and he reacted. He felt inadequate. Moses reacted out of his weakness. But God's response to Moses was "Go. Get going. I'll be right there with you." What God asked Moses to do was to act rather than react. Choose. Decide. Make a conscious choice.

As we have been saying throughout this section, your child will stir you. He or she will stir you to joy, to fear, to frustration. And in the more fearful or frustrating moments, it is easy to fall into the same trap that Moses and that movie theater dad did.

Your daughter calls her little sister "stupid." Your son fails his final exam. He or she pushes you right up to your limit . . . and then pushes again. The easiest thing in the world, in that kind of stirring, is to react and push back. *You* are following *them*. In other words, you turn all of the power in the situation over to your child. And you also hand over your power to choose.

But God says, "Go. Get going. I'll be right there with you." We still want you to listen to the stirrings. But when you react and follow your child, they do the choosing. And it is much harder to be stirred to love when someone else is choosing for you.

How have you found yourself in a cycle of reacting lately? Where are you following your child into him having too much power? What would it mean for you to be stirred to act, rather than react?

Climbing Out of the Baggage

"There was a man from the tribe of Benjamin named Kish. . . He had a son, Saul, a most handsome young man. There was none finer—he literally stood head and shoulders above the crowd! . . .

"After Samuel got all the tribes of Israel lined up, the Benjamin tribe was picked. Then he lined up the Benjamin tribe in family groups, and the family of Matri was picked. The family of Matri took its place in the lineup, and the name Saul, son of Kish, was picked. But when they went looking for him, he was nowhere to be found.

"Samuel went back to God: 'Is he anywhere around?' God said, 'Yes, he's right over there—hidden in that pile of baggage.' They ran and got him. He took his place before everyone, standing tall—head and shoulders above them.

Samuel then addressed the people, 'Take a good look at whom God has chosen: the best! No one like him in the whole country!' "
—1 Samuel 9:1-2; 10:20-24, The Message

Dr. Seuss says, "Today you are You, that is truer than true. There is no one alive who is youer than you."[2] We say, You are chosen. When you were a child, He knew who your child would be. He chose you specifically—because He knew there was none finer. Much like another man that was chosen long ago. He was chosen to be a parent, too, and a king.

It can feel daunting to be chosen . . . quite stirring, actually. As we talk about how you have been specifically chosen to parent your child, it may make you want to disappear . . . just a little. It may make you want to look for your own bag.

Actually, over the course of the next however many years it takes you to raise your child, there will be countless times that the baggage will have some appeal. You will get a call from the school principal to come in "to talk." Your child will ask you about sex for the first time. Your child will lose a friend . . . or find a boy or girlfriend. You may not feel ready to parent in those times. But here you are. You have been chosen. *You have several options. One is that you can hide in the baggage, like our friend Saul. Or you can step out and step into God's good and glorious purpose for you and your child. You are the only you. God has chosen you and you are the best parent possible for your child.*

Artistry

We have a dear friend who is an artist. We've had many moments with her of seeing a new painting she has created and not really having words to respond.

She recently gave a painting to a colleague and friend of ours as a Christmas gift. It was a painting of his two young sons that she'd created from a photograph of the two of them. He opened the gift and immediately tears began to run down his face. He's not the kind of guy who is moved to tears very often, but simply couldn't respond in any other way in this moment. He just sat in silence looking at the picture of his boys and wept. We all watched him and were stirred ourselves.

I had this moment of imagining how often God is moved to tears at the wonder of His creation. Psalm 139:13-16 says that *"you created my inmost being; you knit me together in my mother's womb. I praise you because I am fearfully and wonderfully made; your works are wonderful, I know that full well. My frame was not hidden from you when I was made in the secret place, when I was woven together in the depths of the earth, your eyes saw my unformed body. All the days ordained for me were written in your book before one of them came to be." (NIV)*

I remember seeing my (Dave's) own children for the first time and being overwhelmed by emotion. To see evidence of these tiny beings who were formed in a secret place, and to be overwhelmed by the artistry of our God. There were no words fitting for that moment.

Pull out some of your earliest photographs of your children. Sit and look at those for some moments. If you have video footage of their births, adoption footage, or any early moments in their lives, watch that again. Allow yourself to remember those first moments and what you experienced in meeting your son or daughter for the first time.

Arrows and Warriors

"Sons are a heritage from the Lord, children a reward from him. Like arrows in the hands of a warrior are sons born in one's youth. Blessed is the man whose quiver is full of them. They will not be put to shame when they contend with their enemies in the gate." –Psalm 127:3-5, NIV

Those words are a rich reminder that our children are a gift and we are blessed in receiving the gift. We believe those words also remind us to handle them with wisdom and care. In considering the words about sons being compared to "arrows in the hands or a warrior," and imagining that image, we are called to be intentional people in caring for these gifts. An arrow in the hands of a warrior has the potential for protection and provision. An arrow released without intention and precision has the potential for great harm.

When we release our children into the world without considering who they are, how they were designed and what they need, we are somewhat reckless in our approach to parenting. When we become students of our sons and daughters, we become more thoughtful in our approach to parenting and, in turn, we release them into the world with greater precision and purpose.

Every day, young men and women are released into the world without the care and wisdom we're discussing, and we see the fruit of this. Girls who pursue unhealthy relationships desperately trying to meet a need or an ache that exists in them. Boys who have no purpose, who were never initiated into being a man and are recklessly seeking their own validation and purpose. Young men and women who seem to be wandering aimlessly through life without a clear sense of who they are and living fully outside of who God made them to be.

We've been given a great privilege to release these young, formidable people into the world. We've been given these gifts to handle with care and are called to parent with wisdom and intention.

How would you define your child's temperament from being a student of your child? What are some specific ways that you can creatively work within their temperament rather than against it?

A Note from Paul

*"And of this gospel I was appointed a herald and an apostle and
a teacher. That is why I'm suffering as I am. Yet I am not ashamed,
because I know whom I have believed, and am convinced that
he is able to guard what I have entrusted to him for that day."*
–2 Timothy 1:11-12, NIV

*"This is the Message I've been set apart to proclaim as preacher,
emissary, and teacher. It's also the cause of all this trouble I'm in. But
I have no regrets. I couldn't be more sure of my ground—the One I've
trusted in can take care of what he's trusted me to do right to the
end." –2 Timothy 1:11-12, The Message*

We have talked a lot in this section about fear . . . the fear you
have when you find out you are having a son—or a daughter.
The fear you feel when faced with situations or questions you
don't feel ready to tackle. The fear of walking across the gym
floor, of not being chosen, of not having purpose.

We meet with parents every day in our counseling offices who
are facing these kinds of fears. "How am I supposed to do this?"
is the question that looms behind any and every situation that
brings them to us.

How do I let my child go back to school when he's being
bullied?

How do I help my children deal with a divorce that I can't deal
with myself?

How do I keep them safe on the Internet?

How do I keep them safe from harm?

*Sometimes we believe that the opposite of fear is courage. We would
say that it is not courage, but trust. Parenting would be an impossible
task if it were ours alone. But it is not. You are not alone. You have been
chosen by a God who is more than able. He is trustworthy. And, in the
midst of all of the stirrings and feelings and fears, you can trust Him
with your children. He loves them more than you could ever imagine.
Just as He loves you. And He will keep and care for them—and you—
until that great day when we see Him face to face.*

A Day of Rest

"Oh! May the God of green hope fill you up with joy, fill you up with peace, so that your believing lives, filled with the life-giving energy of the Holy Spirit, will brim over with hope!" –Romans 15:13, The Message

We want you to take this day as a day of rest. Our prayer, today, is that you will find rest and refreshment through Christ. You are in the place He has chosen you to be. God is a God of hope, joy, and peace. May He grant you that today and this week in your journey to raising boys and girls.

Notes:

[1]Madeleine L'Engle, *A Circle of Quiet* (Harper Collins, 1900, 1972), 199.

[2]Dr. Seuss, *Happy Birthday to You!* (Random House Children's Books, 1959), 44.

THE WORLD
OF PRESCHOOLERS

Girls and boys are different. They learn differently. They relate differently. And they develop differently. It's all part of God's design and His plan to make your son and daughter into who He has uniquely called them to be. In this session, we'll begin to explore the differences . . . who they are and what they need in these early, important years of your child's life.

THE EXPLORER
Boys ages 2-4

BOYS ARE WILD, WOOLY, ACTIVE, ADVENTUROUS, CURIOUS, AND EXPERIENTIAL.

THE DISCOVERY YEARS:
Girls ages Birth-5

GIRLS ARE RELATIONAL, ENGAGING, INTUITIVE, AND IMAGINATIVE.

Listening Guide

Icebreaker—
What was
your favorite
costume when
you were a
little boy or
girl?

_____ is foundational for girls across the age groups.

The first stage for girls is called the _____ _____.

She is:

1. _____

2. _____

_____ is the _____ hormone.

3. _____

Imagination creates a fertile soil for _____.

She needs:

1. _____

She needs structure, consequences, and _____, because it helps her feel _____.

2. _____

   There is a trend toward _____ in children.

3. _____

   Girls who are delighted in feel more _____.

Boys in this stage are called _____.

He is:

1. _____

   Boys tend to act first and then _____.

2. _____

   _____ is an expression of _____.

3. _____

He needs:

1. _____

2. _____ _____

   He needs an identified _____ where he can

   take his _____ or frustration.

3. _____

Summary

She walked into my (Sissy's) office wearing jeans, an old T-shirt and tennis shoes that were green on one side and red-and-white-striped on the other. Her mom brought her to counseling because she wasn't being invited to any sleepovers or birthday parties. Her mom was worried. Izzy, on the other hand, was perplexed. She just couldn't understand why the other kids didn't like her. The more we talked about it, the more she realized that it was because she was different.

A few months later, Izzy had reconciled herself to being different . . . and was glad. "I've found a few friends who are different, too. And we can be ourselves together." That May, her class was given an assignment to needlepoint something for their moms for Mother's Day. Most of her classmates needlepointed statements like "I Love Mom," or "Best Mom in the World." Izzy's needlepoint simply said, "Difference is Beauty."

Now if a fourth-grade boy had to needlepoint a gift for his mother (and can you just imagine the damage a fourth-grade boy could do with knitting or needlepoint needles?), his would more likely say "Difference is Cool." And it is. Both things. Out of his infinite wisdom, God designed men and women, boys and girls, to be different down to our very tiniest chromosomes.

Boys are wild and wooly, active and adventurous. Girls are engaging, intuitive, and imaginative. In the words of the famous children's poem,

> What are little boys made of
> Snips and snails and puppy dogs' tails
> That's what little boys are made of.
> What are little girls made of
> Sugar and spice and all things nice
> That's what little girls are made of.

Remind the group that boys and girls will share or even swap some of the characteristics.

Have participants describe what it felt like to find out they were having a son or daughter.

What were they excited about? Afraid of?

RAISING BOYS AND GIRLS

Snips and Snails

Before my (David) daughter was born, someone gave us one of those safety kits to childproof the house—outlet plugs, cabinet fasteners, and so forth. We mistakenly lost the kit in a move we made months before my daughter's birth. I accidentally found the kit while cleaning out our basement two years later and storing some of her delicate, pink baby clothes, in preparation for her twin brothers. I kicked myself for being an irresponsible parent and never remembering to plug up the outlets and safeguard the cleaning supplies from consumption. The truth of the matter is that my daughter never really required that kind of safety plan. I'm not saying that girls don't do their fair share of exploring. They certainly do, but my daughter tended to find objects on the floor, hold them up to us, and hand them over for safe-keeping. It never occurred to her to stick them up her nose, jab them in her ear, or flush them down the toilet.

Her brothers, on the other hand, imagined every one of those scenarios (and then some). There was no safety kit that could have prevented the kind of damage my explorers would bring upon our house—blinds pulled off the windows, toilet lids shimmied off the seat, furniture scuffed. I often say that boys are like puppies. If they are out of your sight and things get quiet, you should be greatly concerned.

Early on, he is a tactile, kinesthetic learner. He explores his world as much with his hands as with his eyes. Parenting an explorer involves creating a safe environment for him to move, explore, experience healthy risk and adventure, and to match his growing curiosity. Parenting an explorer involves paying attention to all the threads of his development—physical, emotional, relational, spiritual, and cognitive. It requires us to pay attention to his unique wiring and to build our expectations, boundaries, responses, discipline, and nurture around his design. We are guilty of parenting in opposition to his design. He needs us to study him and know him.

Sugar and Spice

Girls are relational. You will hear that sentence throughout this study. They are relational in who they are and what they

Look over the following questions together. Suggest that each parent choose to answer a question in the area in which they most need to grow. If you have extra time, they can answer more.

How can you tell that your daughter is wired for relationship? When does your son seem most himself?

How does she invite you to connect with her? How does he invite you to connect with him? How do you respond?

How do you see your daughter/son's imagination at work? Where could you step in and play more imaginatively with them or linger in play?

What kind of boundaries do you have for your daughter/son? Do you need more or less to provide her the kind of security boundaries offer?

Do you let your daughter/son take safe risks? How could you do so more? What are some areas she has opportunity to have courage and he has the opportunity to feel risk?

Do you take the time to delight in your daughter? Do you take time to enjoy your son? What makes it difficult? How could you do more of it?

What are you learning from being a student of your child that you didn't know months ago?

need from us. From her earliest moments, the wiring in your daughter's brain desires to connect. She will connect in the way she looks at you, laughs with you, and smiles. Once she can walk and talk, she will want you to come with her as she discovers the world around her. She will reach out of her little relational being to want to care for you, for friends, even for bugs that are hurt. And she will invite you to imagine with her as you play house, conduct school, and have tea parties. I recently spoke to a father who was worried about his daughter's concern for her stuffed animals. When they picked her up from preschool to leave for a surprise trip to Disney World, she burst into tears. "I can't leave Fluffy and all of my other animals! How would you felt if I went on a trip and left you?"

Because of the importance of their relationship with you, your daughter will need much from you in these first five years. But probably the three most important things she can gain from you are boundaries, a sense of freedom, and delight. She needs to have the freedom to explore the world . . . to wander away within the safety of your care. She needs to be told no, and then she needs to be told yes. As she wanders, she will develop the beginnings of self-confidence. As you stop her from wandering—or disobeying, or hitting her brother—she will develop even more confidence in you and your security. And, finally, you have the tremendous opportunity to delight in her in these years. She longs for you to notice and admire her . . . to think she's wonderful. She wants you to see her as beautiful and smart and funny and all things nice.

Parent Perspective

I (Melissa) have an Explorer puppy. Actually we all do. In the last year-and-a-half, all three of us have lost our old, sweet, calm, predictable dogs . . . and gotten puppies.

My puppy, Blueberry the Old English sheepdog, doesn't look like a puppy anymore. She's a hopping 70 pounds—not whopping, but hopping, because she hops on all fours. Blueberry's hopping wears me out to the point that she has an "aunt" that she goes and has sleepovers with—often.

David's puppy, a yellow lab, is currently 10 weeks old. Just last week, he said he was going to sit Owen on his sidewalk with a sign around his neck that says "Free Puppy." I think that was after Owen went to the bathroom in the office for the third time in one day and catapulted himself onto yet another parent that David was trying to counsel.

Sissy's puppy, Lucy, is a Havanese. She's only seven pounds and waves. Literally. She waves at the kids Sissy counsels. She waves at David. She waves at me. And the instant you stop petting, she starts waving again. With her little bitty paws, she is saying, "Attention makes me happy!"

It's hard to have boundaries, give them freedom, be consistent, and still have the energy to hold up your head to say "good night." Oops! We're talking about dogs, not children. Actually, we would guess you feel pretty similar.

Children in their explorer and discovery years are active, aggressive, curious, relational, caregiving, and imaginative. They need boundaries, open space, consistency, freedom, and delight. You know they need these things, and you even know they will really help. But why is it so hard?

I would say it's hard for a lot of reasons, but there are two that I think are especially difficult in these years. First is the simple fact that you are tired. I met with a parent recently who said, "I know all of the things I'm supposed to be doing. But I work 10-hour days, 4 days a week. I just can't come home and sit and play with my son."

You may not work the same schedule. But you work hard. You work hard to love your child and meet the needs of him or her and the rest of your family. And there are just so many needs in these years. Laundry and boundaries and meals and delight and providing for your family and open space and errands and imagination. And then your child wants to stay up "just a few more minutes." It's exhausting.

Direct the participants toward Melissa's two main challenges for parenting (or puppy-raising) in this stage:
1. Exhaustion
2. Wanting them to be happy

Ask them these questions:

How are you weary right now?

Where do you see yourself giving in to make them happy?

Give them a challenge: Choose one thing to do this week that involves you being a person and not a parent.

There is also the happiness factor. If there is one sentence I hear most often from parents in my office, it's "I just want my child to be happy." He wants to stay up a little longer at bedtime. She wants a candy bar at the grocery. He wants a toy. She wants you to pick her up. And you want your child to feel loved. So, you say, "Okay, just one more," or "This is the last time."

One of the things that happens when you become a parent is that you cease to be a person. You don't get the rest you need. You don't go to dinner with friends or take trips with your spouse. A mom told me a few years ago that she and her husband hadn't taken a trip together in eight years, which was exactly how old their daughter was at the time. Your children need a lot of things, but they don't need to be the center of your universe. That is actually too much attention, which we'll talk about later. They need you to have a life outside of them so you can return to life with them a little more refreshed.

Eugene Peterson said that one of the most important things you can do as a parent is to be a person. You are a person. You are a person who has a son. Or a daughter. Or both. But your son or daughter needs you to get together with friends from time to time. Send your child to his or her aunt's for a sleepover, like Blueberry. Gain some perspective. Know that you are going to be tired. To fail. And that it's okay to give in sometimes. But God gives rest to the weary (Jer. 31:25 and Matt. 11:28) and you are not being a bad parent to take that rest. It's why we have the idea of a day of rest built in to this curriculum. You are a parent and a person. Give yourself room and grace to be both.

~TRY IT OUT~
For Parents of Girls

When we speak at different parenting seminars across the country, we like to ask parents if they think boys or girls are harder to raise. What would your answer be? The general consensus we hear is that boys are harder when they're younger and girls are harder once adolescence starts creeping—or flying—into view.

You can probably guess the reasons. Boys, as David talks more about in his section, have a little more energy (and maybe mischief) in their younger ages. It's those snips and snails and puppy dogs' tails. Girls, on the other hand, are made of sugar and spice and everything nice—until adolescence, that is. Maybe that's when the spice takes a little more effect.

We don't want to scare you parents with girls in these discovery years who haven't yet felt the stirrings of teenagedom in their daughters' lives. We'll come to all of that later. But what we do want to do is prepare you. We want to use this section to start a conversation between you and your daughter that will continue throughout this study and hopefully throughout her life.

So, here's where we want you to start. One of the best things we believe you can do as a parent is to become a student of your child. Get to know her. Obviously, you know more about her than probably anyone else on the planet. But do you really know her? Do you know what she's thinking about when she's quiet at the dinner table? Do you know what she worries about when she can't fall asleep? What brings her the most joy or the most sorrow in her life today? The older she gets, the less likely she volunteers this information. But it doesn't mean she doesn't want you to know. It just means you have to use a little more creativity to find out.

So here are a few questions you could start asking her. We'll talk more in these sections about the context of your conversations at different ages. But, suffice it to say for now that sometimes these conversations flow easier in a relational context. Go for a walk with her. Play her favorite board game. Stay a little longer on the edge of her bed after you say prayers. Wait up for her to come in from the movie with friends. And then ask her a few of the following:

1) How is it different being a girl today than you think it was when I was growing up?

2) What are your favorite parts of being a girl?

3) What do you think the hardest parts are?

4) Do you think boys have it easier or girls? Why?

5) What do you think most girls worry about? What do you worry about?

Obviously, if your daughter isn't speaking yet, or speaking in coherent sentences, she can't answer these questions. But, as young as she can formulate thoughts, you can start the communication going.

For Parents of Boys

It's equally important to become a student of your son. As a parent of twin boys, I am fascinated by the reality that I have these two creatures in my care who have the same genetic ingredients, share gender, were born within minutes of one another, have been raised in the same household, and yet the outcome couldn't look any more different. They are a daily reminder to me of the unique artistry of our God. He has created each of our kids with his own unique blueprint. And it's our job to study that blueprint throughout the course of their lives. Just when you think you have an idea about who he is, he will jump into the next stage of development, and evolve and change as a person. The young man you knew at five years of age will become a different boy at the age of 10. That's not to say that you won't begin to see trends within his temperament as he grows and matures. You certainly will begin to see evidence of his core temperament from the earliest moments of his life. And take note. Our job is to study his temperament and to "train him in the way he should go," as the Scripture so wisely instructs us.

Getting access to his mind and heart is one of the greater challenges in the journey of parenting boys. Within this section of the guide, I'll suggest some questions for you to ask him throughout his development (hang on for some of those in the next chapter). You will need to be strategic in when you ask and how you go about asking. Boys almost have to be tricked into conversation at times. They don't come out of the womb hard-wired with a strong emotional vocabulary. We have to do a good amount of digging and searching. Getting access to a boy's mind and heart is a bit like an archeological dig. There is much evidence to support what we've long known to be true, that a boy typically isn't as verbal as a girl is. He has a more challenging journey of shaping, forming, and using words. There are a number of obstacles to articulating the things he feels in his heart.

Your primary objective in this stage is studying him and beginning the long journey of knowing him. Pay attention to what he enjoys and when he seems most himself. Be willing to linger in play with him for long periods of time. Watch for opportunities to talk around a task (more on this as we go along) as he develops more of an ability to speak and use his words. Allow him to lead in his play, assigning a role to you as a character within his play. His play will be an expression of his heart in this stage.

Acknowledging the limitations in his ability to use his words also means that we want to assist him emotionally. The Explorer feels strong emotions but doesn't know what to do with the emotions, so he will instinctively act on them—hitting, biting, screaming, crying, throwing objects, and melting down. He needs help redirecting his emotions to something useful. He needs us to go with him to a safe place we've set aside for him to take the physicality of his emotions. He needs to hit a pillow or inflatable object, to jump and yell, to lay down and kick. He needs a place to feel the feelings and then some help in putting some words around those strong emotions.

Your son desperately needs you to assess your expectations and your approach to him. He needs the boundaries and your responses to be in tandem with his unique wiring. He needs you to set realistic and achievable expectations for him.

Daily Conversations

Remember the Time

"For you have been my hope, Sovereign Lord, my confidence since my youth." –Psalm 71:5, NIV

When I (Sissy) was in graduate school, one of the assignments they gave us was to write about our earliest memories. Their theory was that there is a reason that your earliest memory is indeed your earliest memory. It speaks to something about you . . . about who you were then, who you are now, and how the environment you grew up in shaped both.

I have two. One is of running in our driveway at an early birthday party and falling. We had one of those confounded aggregate driveways and somehow a rock came unglued and lodged itself in my knee. The next picture in my mind is of sitting on my kitchen counter with my mom bandaging me up.

The other is a scene from our spare bedroom . . . or from life growing up in the 70s, depending on your perspective. My cousin, Blair, had come over to play like he did often. One of our favorite activities was pushing the twin beds together in a V-shape, with each of us taking one bed, one hairbrush and belting out "I'm a little bit country, and I'm a little bit rock and roll" à la Donny and Marie.

Both memories are significant for me because they touch on two important pieces of my childhood. One is the comfort of my mom. The other is a sense of play. Both are still an important part of who I am today.

What about you? What are your earliest memories? What kinds of emotions accompany those memories? What do they say about you? about your relationship with your parents? with others? And how do they affect the way you parent today?

A God Who Delights

"The Lord your God is with you, he is mighty to save. He will take great delight in you, he will quiet you with his love, he will rejoice over you with singing." –Zephaniah 3:17, NIV

I'm (Sissy) not an art therapist. I'm not even an artist. I can draw stick figures, and that's about it. But I love art and have learned about it and how it can be a great tool in therapy from my godmother, who is a very talented art therapist. It is amazing to me the vast stores of information that can be gleaned from crayons. Let's take a drawing of a family, for instance. I ask many girls to draw their family on one of their first visits to my office.

There is one drawing that has particularly stood out to me over the years. It was of a 12-year-old girl who drew a picture of her family gathered around the Christmas tree decorating it. They were smiling and all there in a circle around the tree . . . except for her. She was standing on top of the mantle with her arms outstretched upward, like "Here I am!" If there was a phrase that I would use to describe how this girl felt within her family, it would be delighted in. Her parents did a fantastic job—maybe too good, according to the picture, of making her feel important.

But I want us to go back to the verse in Zephaniah. I want to know where you would draw a picture of yourself in God's family. He would draw you as the one on the mantle. He wants you to feel so loved and delighted in that you would throw your arms up in front of everyone and say, "Here I am!" He rejoices over you with singing. Take the moment that you saw your child smile for the first time, or heard him laugh, or saw her in her first dance recital. Remember the joy that bubbled up inside of you? That is delight. And that is what God feels in you every moment.

With all of this talk about delighting in your child, it may be hard at times, like when he throws up all over your suit before work or when she flings herself on the floor screaming and crying at your parents' house for Thanksgiving. But just as 1 John 4:19 states, "We love because He first loved us." You can delight in your child because Christ delights in you. You are loved deeply, in a stand-up-on-the-mantle sort of way.

Discipline

We are asked questions about discipline daily within our work with parents and almost every time we speak. The topic of discipline drives a number of questions, a range of emotions, and a variety of opinions. As we talk within this stage about setting realistic expectations, defining boundaries, and allowing kids to wander away and return to us, it seems important to begin addressing discipline within our conversation about raising boys and girls.

Perhaps the most common Scripture used within conversations about discipline involves the rod and spoiling. That Scripture stirs the questions, emotions, and opinions we experience when talking with parents around the topic of discipline. The questions stir emotions that give way to opinions about spanking, methods of discipline, and the mechanics of implementing discipline.

We tend to miss the rich instruction about the purpose of discipline that defines the how, when, and why of discipline. *The Message* translates Proverbs 13:24 this way: *"A refusal to correct is a refusal to love; love your children by disciplining them."* The purpose of disciplining our children is to teach them as a means of loving them. And if it is designed as a means of loving our children, our posture in discipline should be one of love, not of anger.

We talk as much with parents about the importance of them taking time-outs as we do about giving time-outs to their kids. Unless we are in a place to discipline in love (and often times our kids' behavior stirs everything but love in us), then we should do whatever we need to do so that discipline can be about teaching, about shaping, and about loving our kids.

A mom I respect said, "I rarely ever discipline without giving myself at least a five-minute 'time out' to really think about what I want to say, pay attention to what's going on inside of me, and pray for wisdom. And let's be honest, sometimes five minutes doesn't touch it!"

That's parenting in love with wisdom.

Loving and Leading

*"Fathers, don't exasperate your children by coming down hard
on them. Take them by the hand and lead them in the way of the
Master." –Ephesians 6:4, The Message*

I've heard a lot of parents yelling lately. I may write a book
called *Parking Lot Parenting,* because it all seems to be in public
places. The father grabs his son by the arm and jerks him out
of the car. The mother yells at her daughter all the way into the
grocery store. These parents are not so well-acquainted with
Paul's words to parents.

Don't exasperate your children by coming down hard on them.
Don't yell at them in parking lots. Don't jerk them. Don't give
excessive punishment or consequences. Don't put your child
down with sarcasm. I know a 50-year-old whose father would
yell at her as she was learning to tie her shoes. "You're not doing
it fast enough! Are you stupid?" To this day, her hands still shake
when she ties her shoes in a hurry.

Don't get me wrong. I know it's easy to get frustrated. Children
in these years don't seem to understand the meaning of the
word *hurry* and the word *no* is questionable. But, God still says
not to come down hard on them. Fortunately, God doesn't stop
there. I don't know about you, but I'm much more of a "tell me
what I can do" person, rather than just what not to do. This
verse gives us two things to help us in raising our sons and
daughters:

1) Take them by the hand. John Calvin said, "Let them be
kindly cherished." God is telling us to have nurturing, intimate,
loving relationships with our children. Hug your son. Take your
daughter by the hand.

2) Lead them in the way of the Master. To parent is to have
strength . . . to be bigger than your child . . . to be an authority.
You are to lead your child.

*In these years, you teach your son and daughter who Jesus is. You
impart your faith to them. You teach them how He lived and how they
can live their lives in response. As you lead them in the way of the
Master, you teach them what that way is.*

Opportunity

We are given so many opportunities in parenting. We began our conversation with Melissa introducing parenting as an opportunity to be stirred and to tap into our own stories. Our friend Dan Allender wrote a book called *How Children Raise Parents*. He discusses parenting as an opportunity for us to grow up as people, to be changed and transformed. Anne Lamott, an author whose work we enjoy, jokingly talks about parenting as an opportunity to connect with our insanity and rage.

We'd say it's all of the above. It's also an opportunity to live the truth of the gospel in front of our kids. Titus 3:4-5 (NIV) states that *"when the kindness and love of God our Savior appeared, he saved us, not because of righteous things we had done, but because of his mercy."* We're given a daily opportunity, in the lives of the kids we love, to live out the truth of that Scripture, to love our kids for who they are. We're called to love them not for what they do, not how they perform academically or athletically, not for how well they behave or what choices they make, but simply for who they are. That's the kind of love and kindness that has been extended to us and how we're called to love. We weren't saved because of great choices we'd made or how we performed as people. In fact, we got the opposite of what we really deserved. We were saved because of His mercy. We have the great privilege of making that Scripture real to our kids when we seek to love and enjoy them for who they are.

Surprise your son or daughter by leaving them a note under their pillow tonight. Write a note reminding them about how grateful you are for the gift of them. Let them discover the note and then read it aloud to them before bed.

Being Small

*"At that time Jesus, full of joy through the Holy Spirit, said, 'I praise
you, Father, Lord of heaven and earth, because you have hidden
these things from the wise and learned, and revealed them to little
children.' " –Luke 10:21, NIV*

When we teach parenting classes, the parents who ask the
most questions are always from the same population. They are
parents of children in stage 1—boys or girls.

As a parent of a young boy or girl, you most likely have a lot
of questions. Do you take a list when you go to the pediatrician's
office? Do you call your mom or friends and say, "When did your
daughter start _____?" You are hungry for any information
that will help you parent your child better. And, honestly, we're
glad. It's why you're participating in this study. Your children will
be glad, too. Information will help you be a better parent.

Information, however, can also make you very overwhelmed.
And this is an overwhelming time as a parent. There is so much
to learn and remember. There is so much for them to learn and
remember. Their brains and bodies are changing rapidly. And
your life has changed just as rapidly.

What Jesus is saying in this verse from Luke is that we can be
too wise at times. It is possible to be too big for God but never to
be too small. Understanding and information can, at times, lead
to pride, to a puffed-up sense that you've got it figured out. You
know how to parent your child right. Don't, in your desire to get
it right, neglect to receive from God.

*God reveals things to little children . . . humble, receptive, dependent
little children. So, rather than putting pressure on yourself to get it
right, allow yourself to be dependent. You may be surprised at how God
reveals Himself to you right where you are. As you're reading your son
the story of Noah's ark, God reminds you of a promise He still intends
to keep. As you pray with your daughter, a co-worker comes to mind
who needs your prayer too. God speaks. He speaks into the heart of a
child, no matter what that child's age. He needs our dependence more
than He needs our wisdom. It's really His wisdom, after all.*

A Day of Rest

"Oh! May the God of green hope fill you up with joy, fill you up with peace, so that your believing lives, filled with the life-giving energy of the Holy Spirit, will brim over with hope!" –Romans 15:13, The Message

We want you to take this day as a day of rest. Our prayer, today, is that you will find rest and refreshment through Christ. You are in the place He has chosen you to be. God is a God of hope, joy, and peace. May He grant you that today and this week in your journey to raising boys and girls.

Notes:

THE WORLD
OF ELEMENTARY-AGE CHILDREN

The differences we identified from the earliest moments of children's lives are accelerated as they grow and develop. Within this next stage of development, we see even more evidence of their growing hearts and minds. During this stage, they begin the elementary school experience. Their cognitive, emotional, and relational worlds become larger and more expansive. We continue to pay attention to who they are and what they need from us. They are absorbing the world around them.

THE ADVENTUROUS YEARS
Girls ages 6-10

GIRLS ARE ADVENTUROUS, SWEET, TENDER-HEARTED, INTUITIVE, AND COMPASSIONATE.

THE LOVER
Boys ages 5-8

BOYS ARE IMAGINATIVE, CREATIVE, ADVENTURESOME, TENDER, AND FULL OF WONDER.

Listening Guide

Ages 6-10 for girls is the stage called the _adventurous_ _years_.

Icebreaker—
What was
your favorite
birthday party
as a child?

She is:

1. _Relational_

Girls will develop a _relational_ strategy.

2. _Fearful_

She needs very _literal_ answers to her _fear_.

Imagination goes crazy

3. _Responsive_ -
   * Compassionate
   * Hungry for truth

She needs:

1. _Opprotunity_

A girl needs a "_North_ _Star_," which is something she feels competent in.

2. _Unity_

She needs you to present a _united_ front.

3. _Grace_

She needs you to become comfortable with the idea of

failure. ← Girls
Internalize
Failure

Boys in this stage are called _Lovers_ Ages
5-8

He is:

1. _Tender_

Ages 5-6 are known as the _Kinder_ years. 7-8
The
2. _Obedient_ Between
years
He genuinely wants to _please_. - Heighten 1 on 1 time
sense of
3. _Competitive_ justice
right + wrong

He needs:

1. _Reprieve_ - Space to - to Move
be a boy
We best wake the male brain up by _movement_. - Primes
brain to
2. _Routine_ Optimal
movement
This is a good time to use _charts_ with boys. - Visual
→media can't spacial
3. _Regulation_ anything self-regulate Learner
with screen
Boys can become obsessively consumed with _media_.

Mid-point check-in for you: How is it going with the group?

Are you doing more of the talking or are they? Do you have one group member who is dominating?

How can you help balance things out more?

Remind them again of the importance of confidentiality, participation, and honesty.

Lead the participants to answer these questions:

How do you see boys and girls differently at this stage? What stands out to you from the teaching so far?

Lead each of them to tell a story illustrating one of the points talked about so far.

Summary

A *Christmas Story* is a film about a young boy growing up in the 1940s, dreaming of owning a Red Ryder BB gun. There's a classic scene where Ralphie and his friends are gathered around a flag pole during recess when a dare is extended. Not just a dare, but a triple dog dare. We watch as Flick accepts the dare, places his tongue on the cold pole and the boys stand in amazement as it sticks. The bell rings and the boys race to class, hoping the situation will magically resolve itself and the teacher won't notice Flick is missing. It's just a matter of moments before Esther Jean, a little girl seated in the front of the classroom, points to a window overseeing the playground and revealing the scene of the crime.

While some of the emotional and relational needs of boys and girls mirror one another, many are different. We will continue to discuss the hunger that stirs in them, how it is within God's very design for the masculine and feminine heart, and how we can attend to that hunger.

A Girl's Hunger

Let's go back to our friend, Esther Jean. Just why is it that Esther Jean was the one who told on Flick? When the teacher tried to find out what happened, the boys just stared straight ahead, trying to look invisible in their desks. But brave and adventurous Esther Jean raised her hand. Why? Because the relationship Esther Jean had with her teacher mattered more to her than being considered a tattle-tale by the boys.

Girls are adventurous in these years. They lack a self-consciousness that will be a constant companion in the next stage of development. If you were to walk upstairs to your daughter's room at this moment, she would likely be drawing her teacher a picture. She might be giving her dog a dance lesson. She could be outside riding bikes with a friend or in the kitchen making a "surprise" for her dad's birthday. But, more than likely, she is thick in the middle of one activity with two objectives—one involving adventure and one involving relationship.

We could just as easily call these years the sugar-and-spice years as we could adventurous. She is living out both characteristics. Your daughter is sweet at this age, much like the "Lover" stage in a boy's development. She is tenderhearted, intuitive, and compassionate. She longs to connect, especially to connect with those she values. She crawls up in her dad's lap to watch a movie. She wants to help her mom make dinner. She draws pictures for her teacher and is just as likely to want a candy bar for her best friend at the grocery as she is for herself. And she does desperately want a best friend. To be invited to a sleep-over makes her heart sing and to be left out of a birthday party is a crushing blow. As in other stages, relationships provide the backdrop for who she believes she is in these adventurous years.

She is also as spicy as she is sweet. She will race a boy in gym class just as easily as she'll climb a tree. Her spirit is as free as her legs in these six to ten years of a girl's life. She is unhindered by fear of what others think. She follows her great big heart to new adventures and relationships. Her spicy-ness can get her into a little trouble in these years, as well. She will toss her head, put her hands on her hips, and try on a little disrespect. The adventurous years are a time for her to test her strengths and her will, in some of the same ways her brother would and some that are quite different. But all of her tests come out of the courage and compassion, sugar and spice, adventurousness and "relational-ness" that characterize these years.

A Boy's Hunger

Along with millions of others across the country, I caught a glimpse of a new Volkswagon commercial during the Super Bowl of 2011. The story follows a little boy, dressed as Darth Vadar, attempting to use "the force" around his house. He makes his best attempt at moving the family treadmill, elevating his sister's baby doll, and levitating the family dog, the washer,

Lead participants to answer the following questions:

Where have you noticed your daughter's hunger for relationship?

When has she gotten her feelings hurt by someone she loves?

Say: In those times, she needs you to sit with her and listen. In doing so, you will validate her hunger for relationship and help her know that what she feels is important.

How could you encourage her compassion?

How can you empower her to take more risks? Where is she taking risks already?

the dryer, and a PBJ sandwich. Upon hearing his father pull in from work, he races outside committed to using his "powers" on his dad's new Volkswagon. As he waves his hands at the parked car, it suddenly starts with the roar of an engine and the lights illuminating. The young boy is jolted in satisfaction and amazement at his abilities. From the kitchen inside, we see his parents smiling at one another as the dad holds the remote that activated the "force."

This commercial brilliantly depicts some truths about the Lover. He is an imaginative, deeply creative, adventuresome little creature. He is tender and full of wonder and amazement at the world around him. It's common to find him in costume or acting on the playful, adventure-based scripts within his growing mind. Boys at this stage of development benefit from having space and freedom to explore in the outdoors; in the safety of their own backyards; and in the castles, forts, clubhouses, and hideaways they will build in their own rooms.

The boy from the commercial, in his desperate attempts to move everything from the family dog to his dad's car, reminds us that a boy has a great hunger for power and purpose. The Lover's play will often center around his playing the hero, the all-star, or whoever holds the most power in the scripts of his mind. He wants to feel powerful and that he has great purpose in the scheme of things.

Our journey of stewarding him will involve assessing the number of healthy opportunities he has to feel purpose and power. We will want to revisit this question again and again. I've long believed that when boys don't have enough healthy outlets to feel purpose and power, they will seek out destructive ways to accomplish that task. We'll talk later about attending to this need in his adolescence.

In this tender stage, we want to flood him with opportunities where he feels his strength and feels a sense of purpose—activities like scouting, outdoor adventures, sports (that are more about having fun, being active, and developing skills rather than highly competitive), and opportunities to volunteer and serve alongside his family where he experiences that he matters and has something to offer others.

How can you help her know that you see her as brave, even if you have a daughter who is shy?

Say: Watch for opportunities to tell her she's been brave or courageous, compassionate, or loving. Every girl continues to want to know that she is delighted in. She hungers for adventure and relationship. She needs you to remind her that she matters and is delighted in by you and by a God who has big, adventurous things in store.

How much time does your son have to engage in play?

Parent Perspective

It's a whole new world. These are the years that your child moves from the safety of home . . . the "predictable-ness" and the consistency that you have created. And they enter the world of school.

School is a transition for so many reasons. There are different types of people, different rules, different games, and so many different things to learn—right off the bat. Many kids enter school with a sense of excitement of all that is to come. But, for some, that excitement can quickly transition into fear or even shame. School also is the first time your child will be measured . . . by someone else. They are given feedback—positive or negative. They are instructed and sometimes criticized. They are graded, even if those grades are smiley or frowny faces. And as *your* child is being graded for the first time, it can often feel like you're being graded as well.

Throughout their growing up, your child will feel, at times, like he or she is an extension of you. You will have trouble differentiating what you feel from what they feel. Their failures will feel like your own, their hurts, disappointments, and their successes. It's a normal part of parenting. But it is also a part that can make things difficult during these elementary school years.

Even the brightest, strongest, kindest children will struggle as they start school. It might be that she doesn't understand a homework assignment. It may be that he is the first to sit down during a spelling quiz while everyone else is still standing. I (Melissa), myself, spent a good amount of time in the coat room for talking in class. Every child will bump up against difficulty and possibly even shame.

Their shame will often take you back to your own. I have seen many parents react to their child from what is obviously their own experience. A father takes his son to the park. The boys are

How often is he given the opportunity to build, create within his room, romp in the outdoors, and use his imagination?

In this stage of his development, where do you see him experience a sense of purpose?

What activities allow him to test his strength, to be active, and to experience validation for his abilities?

If he plays sports, what are the objectives for the league and for his individual coach?

What opportunities for service and outreach could you explore as a family?

How could you expand his opportunities within these areas?

Lead the participants each to answer these questions:

What is one memory from your early years in school? What feelings are associated with it?

Pick one of your children and talk about either how they're like you or different from you.

shooting baskets while his son tries to balance on the bench—by himself. This father reacts, yelling at his son to stop excluding himself and play with the other boys. He was a boy once, himself, who felt left out. A mother whose daughter is taller than the other girls is embarrassed that her daughter is seen as less cute or even lovable and feels her own sense of girlhood shame rise up.

You will have feelings rise up when your child starts school—and throughout these elementary years. Again, we would say pay attention to them. If your reaction feels stronger than the situation warrants, it is a signal that it's more about you than it is about them. And here's what we want you to do:

1) Be aware of your feelings and that they are your feelings, rather than your child's.

2) If you have reacted out of your feelings and gotten angry at your child, apologize. You can even say that you felt left out when you were growing up. They don't need to hear the whole story, but it can help them to know that you struggled, too.

3) Talk to someone you trust—your spouse or a friend.

4) Remember that you are no longer that person. You don't have to feel the spelling test shame or coat room embarrassment any longer. Those experiences don't define you, but God uses them all for His continued glory—in and through you. He can use them to give you a compassionate heart for your child in these elementary years.

~TRY IT OUT~
For Parents of Girls

Several years ago, I (Sissy) was teaching a parenting class on *Raising Girls*. In it, I talked about the Disney princess syndrome. Now, I am a huge fan of Disney, don't get me wrong. It's actually my favorite vacation spot—still. But, I do have some concerns over the fairy tale ending that takes place in almost every story.

Think about it. Cinderella finds her prince. Sleeping Beauty is awakened by a kiss. Ariel gives up her family and fins and everything she knows for hunky Eric. "Happily ever after" is found solely in her finding the man of her dreams.

There is a precious book called *Princess Bubble* that takes the traditional fairy tale to task. The gist of the story is that happy-ever-afters are found in being confident in who God has made you to be and in loving other people. Sounds more like the gospel than a fairy tale, doesn't it?

When I was teaching on this idea and the importance of girls gaining confidence in their identity in Christ rather than a specific relationship or hope for one in the future, one mom in the audience raised her hand. She told me her version—or her husband's version, of Cinderella. These are her words:

"My daughter was going to bed a few months ago. She and her dad had been reading the story of Cinderella together. Night after night, I heard them talking over the baby monitor that sat by her sister's crib. On the night they finished the story, I heard my husband creatively tweak the ending. 'Cinderella met the Prince. They became very good friends. They got to know each other very well and eventually came to love each other very much. They had a royal wedding with all of their friends. For their honeymoon, Cinderella traded her glass slippers in for hiking boots so they could hike all of the mountains in their beautiful kingdom.' " My guess is that he went on to say that Cinderella didn't give up her family but used those hiking boots to visit her mom and dad quite often.

This wise father knew the importance of adventure and relationship in his daughter's life. He spoke to and validated both with his version of an age-old story. He reminded her of the strengths and gifts God has uniquely placed inside of girls. How can you remind your daughter of those gifts? How can you continue to encourage her courage and compassion?

Here are just a few ideas. Take a day trip somewhere she can learn a new activity. Take her fishing. Teach her to water- or snow-ski. Go rock-climbing or hiking and tell her, in the midst of the adventure, how you have watched her love and give of herself to others. Remind her of how brave she is, both in her actions and the way she cares. In terms of relationship, give her opportunities to show kindness to others. Bake a cake together for a new neighbor. Take a meal to a friend who is sick. Have everyone in your family write a note on a holiday to someone who they think might be sad. Rake leaves for a grandparent. Let her not only be involved, but let her even take the lead in to whom and how she can give.

Your daughter wants to know she is loved and delighted in. She wants you to see her as brave and courageous. As you give her opportunities to stretch these strengths that God has already placed inside of her, she will continue to gain confidence in who she is and all that she has to offer . . . and that will continue well beyond these adventurous years.

~TRY IT OUT~
For Parents of Boys

I (David) have been meeting with a young man named Joseph for several months now. Joseph, a first-grader, was bullied by a boy at his school and sometimes finds it difficult to navigate the "triple dog dare" world of boys. Joseph is a great student, has a tender heart and loves reptiles and amphibians of every kind. He lives to visit his grandfather's farm where he typically finds two to three frogs, a snake, and (if he's lucky) a lizard.

I never know who will accompany Joseph when he comes for our appointments. One week it was a frog named Ollie, and one week a lizard named Eddie. He almost always brings an aquarium of frogs and a bag of crickets. While we talk about his experiences at school, we feed crickets to Ollie and his roommates. Although Joseph does well in school, he'd just as soon spend his days with Ollie, Eddie, and the gang, stomping in a creek or exploring at his grandfather's farm. He is everything I love about most boys at this age—tender, curious, adventurous, imaginative, compassionate, engaging, and kind-hearted.

Joseph, like many boys his age, can't self-regulate well and requires a good amount of redirection. He gets lost in a world of imagination and exploration more than he remembers to write his name on his spelling test, finish his chores, comb his hair, or lift the lid. When boys are mean to him at school, he is confused and hurt by their words and actions. He feels things deeply.

He is in the game of life for the fun and adventure. He loves to run and play basketball with his dad. He is fascinated by small things, still loves to read a chapter book with his mom, and he believes his grandfather is one of the most extraordinary men who ever walked the earth. I remind his parents often that, despite the challenges that come with raising boys in this stage, this is about as good as it gets.

As I mentioned before, getting access to a boy's mind and heart is one of the greater ongoing challenges in the journey of parenting boys. I'd continue to recommend the idea of talking around a task. Boys are spatially strong and typically advanced in their gross motor skills. A wise move is to play to these strengths when you engage him in conversation. If you can talk while creating with Legos, feeding crickets to a frog, building a model plane, shooting hoops, or passing a football, he will be utilizing his gifts and talking at times without realizing he is talking. I love to hear moms share stories of having rich conversations with boys while walking the family dog, while later getting access to him over a game of tennis. Dads share stories with me of learning about the things their son is dealing with while throwing a Frisbee at a park or having their son assist them while building or repairing something around the house. These wise parents understand the benefit of talking around a task and avoiding the trap of simply asking questions in the car and getting one-word answers. Some questions you could ask to start the conversation are: 1) *What are the things you think about the most?* 2) *Who is the friend who has been the most loyal to you?* 3) *What are the hardest things about being a boy?* 4) *What do you love the most about being a boy?* 5) *If you could have one superhero power, what would it be and how would you use it?* 6) *Has there been a time that you were courageous enough to stand up for a friend who was being teased?*

Daily Conversations

Like a Child

"For an answer Jesus called over a child, whom he stood in the middle of the room, and said, 'I'm telling you, once and for all, that unless you return to square one and start over like children, you're not even going to get a look at the kingdom, let alone get in. Whoever becomes simple and elemental again, like this child, will rank high in God's kingdom. What's more, when you receive the childlike on my account, it's the same as receiving me.' " –Matthew 18:2-5, The Message

Caroline and Ashley wear tutus when they come to counseling. One is black and one is pink. Sometimes they have on flats with their tutus and sometimes tennis shoes. I've (Sissy) learned that the rest of the outfit really doesn't matter . . . it's the tutus that tell the story. These adorable sisters are both in the adventurous years. They are everything sweet and spicy about this age in a little girl's development. They both have a way of making everyone that encounters them feel loved, mostly because they are so hungry to be loved and enjoyed themselves.

I think that's the simple and elemental part that strikes me about children. They are hungry and there is no question that they are. There is so much that we can learn from the responsiveness of children in these years. There is so much we can learn from their hunger and their openness to Jesus.

Listen to your son talk about what he's learning about God. Watch your daughter as she worships. Ask them why they love Jesus and who He is to them. Have them draw pictures of God or write poems about Him.

Where can your child lead you today? How can you learn from his or her faith? How can you get back to a childlike place in your own faith? To the simple and elemental responsiveness that Jesus calls us to? He is calling you . . .

Spilt Milk

"But because of his great love for us, God, who is rich in mercy, made us alive with Christ even when we were dead in transgressions—it is by grace you have been saved."
–Ephesians 2:4-5, NIV

Last night, we were at dinner with friends who have a son that is a Lover. He is also a burgeoning perfectionist. They told us a story about how angry he got with himself for not being able to kick a soccer ball through a goal the very first time he tried. He yelled and cried and blamed it on everyone standing in the vicinity. As we talked about how to encourage him, his mom said, "I literally remember when I would spill milk at the table when I was growing up. It just wasn't OK. And it's my instinct to respond exactly the same way—even though I know better."

Grace is a need for girls in this stage of development. It is undoubtedly a need for boys, as well. They start to become aware of their failure in these years. We need to talk about that failure. Make it a normal topic around the dinner table. Get ice cream when their soccer team wins or loses. Say, "Oh, well" over their spilt milk. But first, we have say, "Oh, well" to our own.

Easier said than done, we know. You have gotten this far because you know how to push yourself. You have close friends because you work hard at keeping them. You want your children to grow up to be responsible just like you. Your parents expected a lot out of you, and you expect a lot out of your children.

But how are you when you fail? Do you beat yourself up? Are you hard on yourself? Critical of yourself? At camp several years ago, Melissa said, "Jesus doesn't ask us to try harder. Instead, He makes us new." His mercies are new every morning . . . every mistake . . . and every spilt milk. Your son cannot learn those mercies—that sense of forgiveness and grace—until you learn it yourself. He might hear your words but will see something different in the way you treat yourself.

What is an area in your life that you need to accept Christ's forgiveness? He is a God who is rich in mercy and mighty to save. Period. We would encourage you to pray to know His mercies on a daily basis . . . for yourself and for your child.

A Marky Challenge

"What a wildly wonderful world, God! You made it all, with Wisdom at your side, made earth overflow with your wonderful creations." –Psalm 104:24, The Message

"We are on a grand adventure." Marky said these words just after she had been admitted to the hospital for a headache and slurred speech. *Who is Marky?* you might be wondering. She is a friend of ours who has loved all three of us, our families and our dogs for over 10 years. And, just a few short days after the adventure began, Marky was diagnosed with a Stage 4, malignant, aggressive, inoperable brain tumor.

All of us who know Marky are devastated. Prayers and encouragement have come to Marky by email, Facebook message, and regular mail, like letters shooting out of the Dursley's chimney in *Harry Potter.* She has been flooded with love and sympathy from those around her.

But Marky is still on her adventure. On her Caring Bridge site, she posted a picture the next day—the day after she found out about this tumor—of her in the snow. "I had a wonderful walk in the snow last night. I was enthralled by the crystal quality of the snow. The cold air made me feel alive." Marky was diagnosed with cancer and went for a walk in the snow.

Marky's youngest daughter, Amanda, has been by her side constantly. Marky and Amanda are two who have enjoyed each other immensely over the years. Amanda is now in her early 20s and has also been writing on her mom's website:

"Take an opportunity to do something Mom would do this weekend . . . a Marky challenge, if you will. It can be anything. Be adventurous and try something new, show someone kindness, be silly."

In these Lover and Adventurous years, your children live this way quite naturally. We enjoy watching them and the spontaneity they so naturally have. But as we get older, we lose that sense of playfulness. We get too weighted down to live in that kind of freedom. Let's learn from our lovers and adventurers . . . and from Marky. It is a wildly wonderful world He has made, after all. Maybe we can all use a Marky challenge.

Dancing

"You turned my wailing into dancing; you removed my sackcloth and clothed me with joy." –Psalm 30:11, NIV

One of my (Melissa) favorite memories with my mom and brother is dancing. We would all be doing something in the living room—I can't really remember what. But all of a sudden there was music. It didn't matter if it was real or imagined. And we would find ourselves dancing. Dancing and leaping and running in a circle. There was no form. There was no right way to do it. We were just dancing with joy and freedom.

Flash forward to my 12-year-old self. My parents made me take dancing lessons. I can still hear Elvis Presley's voice singing over and over again, "It's Now or Never" and trying to get those steps right. I still hate that song today.

But when I was a girl, dancing wasn't about steps or form. It was an expression of joy. In the Bible, dancing is symbolic of joy as well. When David dances before the Lord, he is expressing his joy.

When was the last time you felt joy? When was the last time you danced? Even laughed from deep inside? Several years ago, I met with a woman who is a trusted spiritual director in our community. We talked for a long time about counseling and it being a helping profession. She said to me, "Melissa, you are giving of yourself every day. You hear sorrow so often that it is imperative that you pray for joy."

You are in a helping profession, as well, as a parent. And you are the primary receptacle for your family's sorrow. They come to you with their hurt, disappointment, and anger. It is hard to feel joy in the midst of carrying such a heavy load. But God wants you to experience freedom. He wants to be the lifter of your head. He wants you to feel joy.

In fact, He wants to turn your sorrow into joy. He wants you to experience that same kind of freedom your son and daughter do as they twirl and run and leap. Pray for joy today. Pray that you can find your joy in Him. You don't have to get the steps right or learn the right moves. You can be free to dance and sing and laugh, as a child of a God who loves you immensely.

The Practice of Presence

"Rejoice with those who rejoice; mourn with those who mourn."
–Romans 12:15, NIV

Years ago, I (David) co-authored a book called *Becoming a Dad: A Spiritual, Emotional and Practical Guide*. It was a book for new and expectant fathers. The book was designed to serve as a sort of road map to guide new fathers along the journey of stepping into parenthood. One of the realities for dads is that we, as males, are wired for activity. We are action-oriented creatures, where women tend to be more process-oriented. There are many different ways that we parent from these strengths within our design as mothers and fathers, and there are ways in which this wiring works against us.

One of the hurdles for many fathers is the practice of presence —simply sitting with our kids in all the moments of life. We tend to embrace the moments of celebration. It's being with our kids in the heartache of life that gets complicated and begins to feel like unfamiliar territory—when our daughters don't get asked to a dance, when our sons aren't chosen for a team, when our kids experience disappointment, rejection, and failure. Our kids need us to rejoice with them and to mourn with them. Many times they don't need us to do or fix anything. They simply want us to be in it with them.

So often we see their disappointment, failure, or heartache as an invitation to intervene. Intervening often communicates to kids that we don't believe they are capable of solving a problem or the pain of dealing with it would be too great for them. Either way, there is a hidden message of "I don't believe in you enough to let you navigate this on your own." We believe that struggle builds great resilience in our kids. Resilience is like a muscle. It's a muscle that needs to utilized and strengthened.

Be willing to mourn with your kids. Celebrate with them when it's time to celebrate. Be in all moments of life with them. Practice the art of being present.

Consider one area where you could take a step back and allow your kids to problem-solve in ways that might bring about growth and maturity.

Does it Hurt?

My son: "Dad, I need to ask you some questions. If Jesus lives in me will He stay for my whole life?"

Me: "Yes, He doesn't come and go. He lives with you forever and promises to never leave you."

My son: "Remember when you talked about the other one— the Holy Spirit one? If He comes inside of me, like you said, is it going to hurt?"

My little guy's question about "the other one" is an accurate picture of where he is in his cognitive development. He is a concrete thinker. The world is very black-and-white. In that moment, he wanted to understand the physicality of what was meant in John 14:16-17, when Jesus said, *"And I will ask the Father, and he will give you another Counselor to be with you forever—the Spirit of truth"* (NIV).

I went on to assure him that there's no physical pain involved in the Holy Spirit entering the body. It didn't involve a surgical procedure of any kind. The truth of the matter is that once my son develops abstract thinking, he will begin to understand that in order for the Holy Spirit to establish residency in me, it did require open-heart surgery. I needed a new heart. And in order for Him to live in me, it means it will hurt. I have hurt more since that heart surgery took place in my life than ever. His presence in me means that my heart breaks and aches over the things I see and experience around me. Because He lives in me, when I see hunger, injustice, or oppression, it grieves me and the Spirit in me. And truthfully, I want to hurt in this way. As believers, we want our hearts to be grieved when we taste the heartache of living in a fallen world.

My son feels that ache already. He has tasted the reality that not all things will be made right this side of heaven. My job is to walk with him and demonstrate what a life of faith looks like on a grown-up. That's a weighty responsibility.

Consider today what your son or daughter sees when they observe a life of faith on you as an adult. How would they define what it means by watching you—not listening to your words, but listening to your life?

A Day of Rest

"Oh! May the God of green hope fill you up with joy, fill you up with peace, so that your believing lives, filled with the life-giving energy of the Holy Spirit, will brim over with hope!" –Romans 15:13, The Message

We want you to take this day as a day of rest. Our prayer, today, is that you will find rest and refreshment through Christ. You are in the place He has chosen you to be. God is a God of hope, joy, and peace. May He grant you that today and this week in your journey to raising boys and girls.

Notes:

Emma
* Needs to discuss failures
as well as praise success

Needs Chart

THE WORLD OF EARLY ADOLESCENTS

It has been said, for many years, that girls mature faster than boys. This is the session when it becomes most obvious. Boys are still coming down from The Lover stage. They are seeking to understand themselves and engage in the world around them, but they want and trust you to help guide them in the process. They are individuating, but they want to individuate while still being connected to you as their parents. Girls have taken their adventurousness and run with it—and are often, it feels like, running as far away as possible from you and from who they were just a few short years (or months . . . maybe days?) ago.

THE NARCISSISTIC YEARS:
Girls ages 11-14

GIRLS ARE INSECURE, MOODY, EMOTIONAL, AWKWARD, AND FOCUSED ON SELF.

THE INDIVIDUAL:
Boys ages 9-12

BOYS ARE GROWING IN STRENGTH, NEEDING RESPECT, SEARCHING FOR THEIR IDENTITY, AND FACING TEMPTATION.

Listening Guide

This stage for girls is called the _Narcisstic Years_

_____.

She is:

1. _Relational_   , critical   - miss social cues
   - wanting a group

   Relationships are what bring her the most _joy_

   and the most _pain_ _____.

2. _Insecure_

   10-11
   Growth Surges

   The two things that her rapid brain development affects are

   her _memory_ and her _confidence_ .

3. _Ambivalent_ -

She needs:

1. _Space_ to _Grow_

   She needs _privacy_ and time to develop who she is.

2. _Strength_

   She needs you to be _Stronger_ than she is.

3. A _Back Door_

   To the degree that kids can _predict_ you, they

will _**dismiss**_ you.

Ages
9-12

Boys at this stage are called _the individual_.

He is:

1. Searching

   Boys are primarily searching for _Identity_ and

   Masculinity. ← Consumed with ranking
   in pecking order
   -Critical of others

2. Evolving

3. Experimenting

   He is experimenting with _profanity_ and

   breaking the _rules_. Boys

   crave _power_ and _purpose_.

He needs:

1. Involvement - Supervision

2. Information

3. Outlets

   He needs outlets to test his _Strength_, test

   his _mind_, feel _risk_ and adventure,

   and feel _purpose_.

Summary

They sat on the couch opposite us. David and I each were in chairs, armed with all of the wisdom we hoped to offer this brother and sister who were once again at odds . . . and at very loud odds, we should say.

Their mom asked us to meet with them together. We had done so several times over the past few years since their parents' divorce. We had gone over ways to help them get along better, code words they could use to take a break when one or the other was escalating, and activities they could do together to strengthen their relationship. But here we were in the midst of their fighting—all over again.

We do need to include the fact that Josh is in the Individual stage. He is funny, a little subversive with his sister, and wiggly at 11 years old. Jennifer is in all of her narcissistic glory at 13. She feels awkward in her own skin, and that awkwardness comes out in the way she sits, the way she talks, and the way she regularly rolls her eyes at her brother.

As we talked through their last argument, Josh was quick to say, "Jennifer stops before I do. She knows how to walk away." (Still the sweetness of the Lover stage bleeding through.)

"Yes, I do," said the all-knowing Jennifer.

As she added her mental points to the scoreboard, he spoke up, "But she won't wake up on time, and she makes me late for school. She spends hours in front of the mirror. And then I get mad. She thinks everyone's supposed to do what she wants."

"No I don't," Jennifer interrupted. "It takes girls longer to get ready. I don't expect someone who barely combs his hair to understand that."

We decided to hit the pause button before World War III ensued. It's easy to see how these two could get stuck, both defending their positions.

Have the participants reflect on:

What are the strengths in this stage of development for boys? for girls?

What are the challenges for boys? for girls?

What do you want to hang on to from the teaching on this stage?

Through Josh's words, you can hear him wanting to assert himself. He wants to be respected. He is growing in strength, but still has enough of kindness to see his part in the conflict. He has stepped out of the Lover stage and into the Individual. There is evidence still of where he's been. We see lingering elements of the tender, obedient, relational little guy we knew, while witnessing evidence of a young man in search of his identity, and attempting to find his voice.

This next stage of his development involves him wrestling with his sense of himself. By 9 to 10, a boy's brain is beginning to look deeply into what it means to be a man. He is curious about all things masculine in ways he simply couldn't be before. He is evolving and beginning to change. While girls continue ahead in the development race, and will begin experiencing changes in their bodies earlier and at a more advanced pace, he will trail behind with a slower, more gradual evolution.

He will experiment more with breaking the rules outside of home and needs us to be invested, involved, and aware. This is the most common window for a boy to have his first exposure to Internet pornography. He needs safeguards on the technology he has access to within our home and beyond. Equally so, he needs us to be strategic and diligent in our parenting, asking great questions when he spends time at other homes, and working to safeguard his heart and mind.

He needs us to flood him with information about his changing body, and the emotions that accompany those changes. As he edges toward adolescence, we want the Individual to feel armed and informed. We don't wait on the changes to take place and then give information. We want to stay a step ahead of his development. Puberty needs to be put in a physical, emotional, and spiritual context.

Equally important is that he have experiences in relationship with us where we are simply enjoying him for him. We aren't just celebrating good grades (achievements) or game victories (performances), but simply celebrating the way God made him and participating in the things he loves to do. We want times with the Individual that are void of instruction, discipline,

Lead the participants to answer the following questions:

Are you having an ongoing conversation with your son about his growing body, his developing emotions, and understanding relationships with the opposite sex?

What safeguards do you have in place within your home to safeguard his mind and heart? What are your family rules on media and technology?

What are two to three things your son enjoys within this season of his development? Set aside time to be about those things with him.

teaching, or shaping. Those are all important ingredients, but he needs times with us that don't involve those elements.

Jennifer doesn't quite know what to do with herself. She has one foot tentatively placed in childhood and is doing her best to stomp her other into adulthood. She doesn't know who she is and sure doesn't know who to be. The hours she spends in front of the mirror are just a reflection of the insecurity she feels in not only the way she looks on the outside, but also in who she is on the inside.

Girls, in these years, are emotionally all over the map. In our book for girls, *Mirrors and Maps,* we compared them to the Tasmanian Devil from the Warner Brothers cartoons. They have hormones surging through their brains and bodies. They have the hiccups in confidence that we talked about in the video. They come into most rooms spinning and take everything and everyone up in the swirling process. Narcissistic Years girls have a lot working against them. And so what do they do with all of the chaos and confusion they're feeling? You already know the answer, if you have a daughter in these years. They often take it out on you, as their parents.

We have had literally countless parents over the years say some version of the same comment: "I don't know what happened. Yesterday, she was all smiles and would crawl up on my lap to watch TV. Today, she doesn't want to be seen with me. She is angry at us and embarrassed by us constantly. It's like a switch was flipped and she changed overnight."

It is the most frightening episode of life you and she will experience. But she needs you to hang in there with her. She will push against you with all of the strength that she has in her little ambivalent self. But she is pushing against you because she wants to know that you won't move. She needs your consistency. She needs your kindness and your belief in her even when she is being the worst version of herself. She needs you to choose your battles but still provide consequences for the biggie. She needs you to enjoy her. And she needs you to continue to delight in her so that you and she can both remember that there is something delightful in her—even when it feels difficult to see.

Parent Perspective

What is your favorite channel on the radio? Recently, I've started listening to XM radio. XM is much more gracious to aging music . . . and aging people. Instead of an "Oldies" station, they name their stations by decades. The 40s are simply called the 40s, not uber-oldies or anything like that. My favorite happens to be the 60s. I turn on the radio and immediately start tapping my toes. The music just makes me feel good.

A song comes on and I am transported. The other day, I heard the beginning strains of "dee doody doom doom" and was sitting, not in my car, but in my friend's aunt's car on the way to Florida. I was 12 all over again, with my three friends singing as loudly as we can, "Seven little girls sittin' in the backseat huggin' and a-kissin' with Fred."

I would guess music does the same for you. It takes you back. You may not be able to remember which president was in office or which history class you took in 6th grade, but you can remember every word to a particular song. You hear the opening notes and your mind is flooded with memories . . . where you were, who you were with, even what you had on.

Since being reminded of Fred and the girls in the backseat (which is, now that I think about it, a little concerning), I've been wondering why it is that our memories are so vividly tied to music—and particularly to music from early adolescence. The answer that makes the most sense to me is emotion.

Our early teenage years are undoubtedly one of the most emotional times of our lives. In these years, we felt every bit of the heights of joy and the depths of extreme sorrow. You can see it in your children today. A mom of 12-year-old twins brought them in for their first counseling session and said, "Well, their names are Allison and Catherine, but we call them Trauma and Drama." Boys and girls are dramatic and experiencing trauma, each in their own way. We were, too. And it takes only a few bars of our favorite songs from those times to take us back.

Identify an area (academic, athletic, chores) where you can take a step back, creating more opportunity for your son to develop responsibility or strengthen his resilience and allowing you be less involved.

If your daughter has already moved into the narcissistic years, what was the transition like for you? for her?

Where do you see her insecurity?

What are some characteristics you see in her (even in her narcissism) that you could remind her of?

What does she enjoy?

How could you enjoy some of those things with her?

Where do
you need
to be more
consistent?

Where and
to whom are
you able to
talk when
things get
hard with your
daughter?

What are you
learning about
yourself so far?

Share a time
you've reacted
recently. What
could you
have done
different?

Teaching
Tip: The
participants
may not
all want to
answer the
questions,
which is OK.
They may
need you to
answer first,
to help them
feel more
comfortable.

Ask the
parents
to share
resources and
ideas about
talking to
kids about
puberty and
their physical
development.

But we can also be taken back in other ways. Your daughter is getting ready to try out for cheerleading. You seem to be more invested in her getting her round-off back-handspring than she is. Maybe it's because you still remember the pain you felt when you tried out and didn't make it. As a kid, you never felt your dad's approval. No matter how poorly or well you played in a basketball game, your dad had something negative to say. And, now, you have a son with a lot of talent. You push him—sometimes too hard, but it's just because you don't want others to criticize him the way you were criticized.

We remember the joy and the pain of our early teenage years . . . maybe especially the pain. As a parent, these are the years that can really challenge your perspective the most, because your past can color that perspective. It can make you push or protect your child more than you would have because of your experiences when you were his or her age. What memories are being stirred up in you in these years? What songs take you back and what do they take you back to? How do you move on from a past that was so painful that it feels like yesterday, rather than 15, 20, or even 30 years ago?

One of the primary differences in you and your child is your ability to act. They are often, in these years, simply reacting. They're often not really in control—of their emotions or their decisions. Someone hurts them and they hit or hurt back. You ground them and they roll their eyes. They are impulsive and reactionary as a part of their makeup as teenagers.

But you are no longer bound by that impulsivity. You don't have to react out of the pain of your past. You can choose to act. You can choose to parent them differently than you were parented. You can treat them differently than you were treated. And we have a few suggestions that might help:

1) Pay attention to the memories that are stirred in you.

2) Identify and talk about the feelings with someone you trust.

3) Pray that God will help you see yourself as you are now—as a parent armed with God's wisdom and truth, who is free to love and act, rather than simply react.

4) Read "Coming Alongside" in the "Daily Conversations" section.

For Parents of Girls

"To the degree that kids can predict you, they'll dismiss you." These words are the first sentence in the book that Melissa and I wrote, *The Back Door to Your Teen's Heart*. They're also the words that describe the conversations in countless cars across the country every afternoon.

You pick your 12-year-old daughter up from school. "How was your day," you congenially ask.

"Fine," she grunts.

"What did you do in school today?"

"Nothing." Another grunt.

And there you have it. You're not only dismissed but left with silence for the entire car ride home.

With teenagers, that's what happens when you come through the front door. (These same ideas will hold true for boys in the next stage of their development.) Figuratively, and sometimes literally, you get the door slammed in your face. More examples of the front door involve statements such as, "Let's spend some quality time together." "We haven't talked in a while. Tell me what's going on in your life." You get the picture.

So let's think about coming in through the back door. Choose something she loves and feels like she knows a lot about. Tell her how much you value her opinion (even if it's mostly just in this area). You can have her help you go through your closet and get rid of old clothes, if she loves fashion. She could teach you how to use a certain feature on your cell phone. She could help you set up or update your Facebook page. If you ask her to help you, she will feel a little power and a little respect, two things she's craving in this stage of life. And she will also feel important—something she doesn't feel very often in these years. (We promise she doesn't, even though she acts as if the world revolves around her.) Then, as you're going through the closet,

> **Challenge: In this next week, attempt to have a back door moment with your son or daughter. Come back and share that moment with the group.**

you can ask her about the party she went to the night before. Or, sitting at the computer together, you can ask her how it's going with a friend she was having trouble with. And, all of a sudden, she finds herself talking to you because she doesn't think she's supposed to. That's the back door.

What does it look like for you to connect to your daughter in a way that is both unpredictable and relational? For me, the back door doesn't come naturally. It takes forethought on my part. It might on yours, too. And, by the way, unpredictability doesn't equal inconsistency in your parenting style. You can still be direct and concrete in her discipline. She needs you to be. She needs predictability in her consequences and your strength as a parent. But you invite conversation and relationship when you wander unpredictably through the back door.

~TRY IT OUT~
For Parents of Boys

My sons are currently playing in a basketball tournament. It's our local version of March Madness. It's a double elimination tournament, and our team has made it to Day 3 with only one loss. By the close of today, we'll have either been eliminated or crowned the champions. Needless to say, adrenaline and testosterone permeate my home. My wife can hardly wait for this event (she agrees with the "Madness" part of the title) to come to a close.

We stepped into the gymnasium yesterday and the place smelled of basketballs, bleachers, sweat, and all things boy. The room was full of young athletes, racing up and down the court, fighting for a victory. The bleachers were filled with parents, grandparents, siblings, friends, and fans who'd devoted their weekend to the young men on the court. Some of the adults came to cheer, some of them came to celebrate, some came to support, and most came with cameras and videos. Everyone seems hopeful for a victory for their team—a chance to advance on to the next bracket.

We arrived early to meet up with our team, and I had a chance to watch while my boys talked strategy with their coaches and teammates. The teams playing before us were of the same age but more advanced in their skill and ability. Their parents appeared to be more advanced in their skill and ability as well. I say this because despite each team being equipped with coaches, this group of parents (as is often the case) felt a need to coach from the sidelines. While the coaches were calling out plays from one side of the court, the parents were doing the same from the other side. One young man looked distressed as his coach yelled to him from the east side while his dad leaped off the bleachers and combed the boundary yelling at him from the west side. When the referee called a foul on one of his teammates, this dad started stomping and screaming at the referee (who I'm guessing to be 15 years old).

I once counseled a young man who experienced his own version of the scene I just described. He was dribbling near the sidelines, trying to remember the play, attend to which of his teammates was open, dribble the ball despite a full court press, all while his coach yelled from one side and his dad from another. The intensity became too great and this third grader stopped dribbling, held the ball and screamed, "Will everyone please stop yelling at me? I'm trying to think."

Three rules to keep in mind:

1. If we turn our sons over to capable coaches and educators, it's our job to become cheerleaders. He needs enjoyment and support, not to be flooded with instruction.

2. Athletic experiences are designed to teach boys skills, encourage sportsmanship, keep boys active, and provide a context for problem-solving, experiencing victory and defeat, being a part of team, and most importantly, having fun. It's about him and not about us.

3. One of our objectives is to teach boys to disagree with others with respect. When we rail against referees and coaches from the sidelines, or a teacher in the hallway, we're modeling something different from what we are asking of boys.

Daily Conversations

Sheep Among Wolves

"Stay alert. This is hazardous work I'm assigning you. You're going to be like sheep running through a wolf pack, so don't call attention to yourselves. Be as cunning as a snake, inoffensive as a dove."
–Matthew 10:16, *The Message*

Matthew 10:16 is the verse with which we start off our book, *The Back Door to Your Teen's Heart.* It explains the concept—in very different terms. Rather than Jesus sending out the disciples, it is our version of sending out you, right back into your homes. One of you is the sheep and one of you is the wolf. Guess which is which? You guessed it. You are the sheep running through a wolf pack. Tweens, pre-teens, and teens all have several things in common with wolf packs. They stick together. They often don't think for themselves but follow each other into whatever the alpha/mean girl/cool guy says. They can be snarly and snippy whenever they want.

As for you, we do know you're much smarter than a sheep. But we're also sure you have some sheep-y moments as a parent. You don't understand why, but the wolves just keep snarling and circling. So what's a sheep—or parent—to do?

You want to be inoffensive, dove-like, tender, connected, relational—as much as they'll let you. But then, they need you to be cunning. Give them consequences. "I will not let you talk to your mother that way because I believe that you are a much kinder, respectful young man than you're acting right now." "You will make up your little brother's bed for a week, since you seem to want to be his mother already." Parent in ways that are as cunning as a snake. Be unpredictable. But be relational at the same time.

Hold his hand. Point your finger. Be as wise as a serpent and gentle as a dove. Love her through the back door and all the way through the chaos of these tween/pre-teen/teenage years.

Unity

Many years ago, I (David) took my sons to a camp in North Carolina hosting a father/son weekend. As you step onto the campus of this refuge for boys, there is a sign hanging over the main hall that reads "Behold, how good and how pleasant it is for brothers to dwell together in unity." The words are from Psalm 133:1 (NASB). My wife took an art class years ago and took that Scripture and created a beautiful piece of art that hangs in my son's room. The art was created with paint, old vintage pieces from our family's history, and those rich words.

In case you are wondering, my boys don't always live in unity with one another. In fact, some days there is little evidence of unity in their relationship. Boys (males of all ages) struggle with collaborating when they are instinctively wired to compete. Regardless, we continue to pray those words over their room, over our home and over the people who share life within that space. We are hoping to live with an awareness of what it means to model unity for our children.

For my wife and for me, unity means that we have a common spirit. We want the same things. Because of the differences that exist in us because of our gender, our temperaments, and our styles, the execution of parenting looks different. Some days not all that different, some days very different. But what we hope our children experience is that we share the same values, the same core beliefs, and the same desires for our children, our marriage, and our family.

We are hoping to model what it means to disagree with respect and to respond with kindness, compassion, humility, self-control, patience and gentleness. Unity for us means that we can come at something with a completely different perspective, and somehow manage to honor, celebrate and support the other person. It means we can disagree and come back together if we need to apologize, take ownership for our part and do whatever is needed to repair the relationship.

Define unity with your kids at some point this week. Consider writing a mission statement for your family, identifying the core beliefs of your family, the principles you prioritize and what defines you as people who share life together.

The Power of Like

*"Three things amaze me, no, four things I'll never understand—
how an eagle flies so high in the sky, how a snake glides over a rock,
how a ship navigates the ocean, why adolescents act the way they
do." –Proverbs 30:18-19, The Message*

"What was he thinking?"

"I can't imagine what's gotten into her head!"

"Why in the world . . . ?"

Have you found yourself asking any of these questions in the
last few days/months/years—basically since your child has been
moving toward teenagedom? We would guess the answer would
be a resounding "Yes!" The writer of Proverbs wondered the same
thing. Often, as David Thomas says, when you're wondering
what they're thinking, the answer is that they're not.

Girls in this stage and boys, beginning now and moving into
the next stage, will have some of their very least enjoyable
moments. It will be profoundly difficult to connect to them.
He gives one-word answers. You walk up the stairs to talk and,
just as you reach the top stair, she shuts her door. You can't go
see movies together because he doesn't want to be seen in the
same 50-foot radius as you. You can't watch television with her
because you're just not particularly interested in the secret life
of any American teenager except hers.

And we still say enjoy them.

It doesn't mean you have to understand them. Donald
Miller, in *Blue Like Jazz*, said, "Nobody will listen to you unless
they sense that you like them."[1] So, enjoying them really
accomplishes two purposes with teenagers.

1)It fosters a relationship that is often tenuous.

2)It makes them a little more willing to listen.

*If she loves a certain band, have her play you some of her favorite
songs and tell you what she loves about them or the lyrics. If your son
loves Lord of the Rings or some other boy-like killing-monsters movie,
watch it with him and find out what draws him to it. If you learn about
anything they love, in these years, you learn about them. You may not
learn to understand them, but maybe you can communicate a little of
how much you like—and love—them in the process.*

Fear and Courage

"For God did not give us a spirit of timidity, but a spirit of power, of love and of self-discipline." –2 Timothy 1:7, NIV

Melissa Trevathan, among her many gifts, has the gift of creativity. She has this remarkable ability to make the truths of Scripture real and digestable for people of all ages. For as long as I've (David) known her, I've watched her wander in front of a group of kids, teenagers, or adults, carrying some random object—a rock, a suitcase, a rotted piece of fruit, a glass of water, a plate of pancakes—and wonder where she will be taking us.

After spending a first summer at our Daystar camps, my own daughter came home with some rich truth wrapped around her mind. My daughter was moving schools that fall, weeks after her experience at camp. We talked often about how she was feeling about her first day at an unfamiliar place. Our conversations about this new chapter changed after camp. She'd say things like, "Miss Melissa said courage isn't the absence of fear, but the presence of fear. Being afraid isn't so bad if it means I have a chance to be courageous."

She begin to think differently about starting a brand new school, speaking in front of a group of people, trying something new for the first time. She still feels nervous, timid, afraid, and sometimes even terrified in the face of those opportunities. But she understands fear presents the opportunity for courage. And that God hasn't given her a spirit of fear or of timidity, but one of courage. She is growing in an understanding that those feelings don't define her, they are just that . . . feelings. And she can offer those feelings, and all the ideas that accompany them to a God who cares about the way she feels and the intimate details of her life.

Melissa challenged us as we jumped off in this study to parent out of love and not out of fear. That takes a great amount of courage. We've all been given a spirit of power and love.

Take the advantage of having a dinner conversation around courage. Ask family members to identify a time they felt courageous in the face of fear. Consider having everyone identify a particular struggle or challenge they have faced and how it gave way to some opportunity to give to someone else.

Coming Alongside

"All praise to the God and Father of our Master, Jesus the Messiah! Father of all mercy! God of all healing counsel! He comes alongside us when we go through hard times, and before you know it, he brings us alongside someone else who is going through hard times so that we can be there for that person just as God was there for us."
–2 Corinthians 1:3-4, *The Message*

Pick one popular song from your individual or narcissistic years. What is the first song you learned to dance to? That you remember listening to with a group of friends singing? That was playing on the radio when your dad took you fishing? Find that song. If you have access to the Internet, you can find it on *Pandora.com* or iTunes. If you don't have access to the Internet, sing as much as you can of it yourself. What memories are associated with it? What were you doing? Who were you with?

As you think back, allow yourself to remember some of the other happy memories you have of that time. Who were they with? What sounds and pictures—even smells—go along with them?

What are some of the more painful memories? Do you remember feeling left out? Betrayed? Hurt? Insignificant? Maybe even invisible? As you think back on those times and all of the emotion that was inside of you, where was God in it? How did He come alongside you in those years, in that pain? Who did He use, how did He comfort you, how did He speak truth into your heart? How has that truth had an impact on who you are today?

Today you know the Father of all mercy. If you don't, it's as simple as talking to Him. He longs to bring healing to the places that still hurt. He has been coming alongside you since the day you were born and will continue to in His great mercy. He loves you and longs to be the God of all comfort to you. Then you, in turn, can come alongside your son who feels like a failure. You can walk with your daughter who wants so desperately to feel that she matters.

He comes alongside you so that you can come alongside them . . . even if it's in a back door way. He is the God of all mercy and all comfort, and He is a God of hope. Always. Whether we're 13 or 30 . . . or a 30-year-old who still, on some days, feels 13.

An Opportunity to Grow

"Growth is the delight of the child and the agony of youth, but it is not natural to the middle aged." –Eugene Peterson[2]

This growing up process is not natural . . . at least it's not for you. Children, tweens, and even teenagers are always looking toward something.

"I can't wait to be double digits."

"Well when I turn 13 . . . or 16, 17, 18 . . ."

We, on the other hand, are not looking toward so much anymore. We may be looking back. We're hopefully looking here . . . at what's right in front of us. But we don't have quite the excitement about growing older that our children do. And you may not really even be looking forward to their growing up. At best, it's bittersweet. You wouldn't want them to have to live in this pre-adolescent awkwardness forever. But you were really hoping this stage would hold off for as long as possible.

In the beginning of this section, we talked about this being the most frightening episode of life for a girl and her parents. For boys, the frightening part is just starting to raise its head—and your heart rate—in these years.

When we talked about what we wanted to name this curriculum, *Grow* is one of the names we considered. Raising boys and girls is about their growth—and yours. And in these years, particularly, you have a tremendous opportunity for growth.

Eugene Peterson goes on to call adolescence a gift in the life of a parent. It may not feel that way right now. The idea of adolescence may be met with much more trepidation than excitement for you. But we promise there can be good gifts along the way. God can use this time, while He is growing your son or daughter, as an opportunity to grow you, as well. What does or could that growth look like in your life today?

Father, we pray that You would be near to the parents who are reading and working through this curriculum today. Bless their children with the knowledge of Your grace and unbounding love for each of them. And open their dads' and moms' eyes to how You specifically, lovingly want to be growing them, too—as parents and as people. Amen.

A Day of Rest

"Oh! May the God of green hope fill you up with joy, fill you up with peace, so that your believing lives, filled with the life-giving energy of the Holy Spirit, will brim over with hope!" –Romans 15:13, The Message

We want you to take this day as a day of rest. Our prayer, today, is that you will find rest and refreshment through Christ. You are in the place He has chosen you to be. God is a God of hope, joy, and peace. May He grant you that today and this week in your journey to raising boys and girls.

Notes:

[1]Donald Miller, *Blue Like Jazz* (Thomas Nelson, 2003), 220.

[2]Eugene Peterson, *Like Dew Your Youth: Growing Up with Your Teenager* (William B. Eerdmans Publishing Company, 1994), 7.

THE WORLD OF LATE ADOLESCENTS

The gap is widening. The girls, in this stage of their development, have basically lapped the boys. They are leaving the self-absorption of the teenage years behind, while the boys are thick in the middle of it. Boys are wandering. Girls are arriving . . . or at least arriving at the beginnings of their adulthood. The wandering that boys will experience, in these years, will be somewhat difficult to watch. But let the girls serve as a reminder. He will get there . . . it just takes a little more time . . . and maybe a lot more patience.

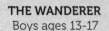

THE WANDERER
Boys ages 13-17

. . . .

BOYS ARE ARROGANT, ARGUMENTATIVE, INSECURE, VOLATILE, AND STRUGGLING WITH IDENTITY.

THE AUTONOMOUS YEARS
Girls ages 15-19

. . . .

GIRLS ARE RELATIONAL, EXPERIENCING BODY CHANGES, INDEPENDENT, EXPRESSIVE, NEEDING MORE FREEDOM.

Listening Guide

Icebreaker—
Share an
awkward
adolescent
moment.

Stage 4 for girls is called the _____

_____.

She is:

1. _____

    These are the years when _____ becomes much

    more of an issue.

2. _____

    As girls get older, they get _____.

    Eating disorders are about two things: _____

    and _____.

3. _____ _____ _____

    We want them to have _____.

She needs:

1. _____

2. _____ to _____

You want to _____ the _____

incrementally.

3. _____

A boy at this stage is called the _____.

He is:

1. _____ _____ _____

He is experiencing between 5-7 extra surges of

_____ a day.

2. _____ and _____

His arrogance is a cover for his _____.

3. _____

He needs:

1. _____ _____

2. _____

3. _____

He is an experiential _____.

You need a parenting _____.

Lead the participants to share their back door moment from the past week.

Read aloud Luke 15:11-32. Encourage each parent to share how they see their son or daughter in the story.

Share these suggestions for parents of sons:

You will want to become more creative and strategic in how you engage him. Keep considering the "back door" approach for how to connect and communicate with him.

Identify three strengths you see in him and call those out with regularity.

Summary

Traditionally at Daystar Counseling Ministries, we have kept the boys' and girls' group meetings separate, except on the rare occasion when we gather to discuss something like "Why in the world boys/girls act the way they do." But, one year, several years ago, the three of us decided to try something different. We wanted to try a co-ed leadership group. This group would be made up of some of our most mature high school boys and girls. They were a part of our "leadership team" at Daystar—a group of kids we handpick to help lead our younger kids' groups and camps. This leadership group would meet every Thursday night.

So, one Thursday night in September, we had our first group. It was made up of five girls and four guys. That first week, the guys were obviously the most nervous. Their feet shuffled and eyes shifted around the room uncomfortably. The girls, as you could guess, were a little freer. They laughed easily with each other, having been in group together for some years. They tried their best to make the boys feel comfortable, asking them questions to draw them out. It didn't really work. After group, the three of us talked for a few minutes. We chalked up the girls' talkativeness and the boys' lack thereof to first-week jitters.

The next several Thursdays, it was the same scenario. Maybe a sentence or two more than the week before, but the fact was that it just wasn't going to work. The wandering boys were awkward and rendered almost speechless by the presence of these mature, expressive, autonomous girls. And that was the end of our co-ed counseling groups at Daystar.

A guy desperately wants to feel comfortable in his own skin, but he just doesn't. This stretch of development is plagued with physical, emotional and relational change. He will be the worst version of himself at some point (if not in *many* moments) in this stage of his development.

I believe the young men from the group wanted to offer more to the group, but they couldn't quite get past themselves. As boys in this stage wrestle with their sense of identity, they are trapped in insecurity. A boy at this age tends to mask that insecurity with arrogance and bravado. He is a man of extremes in this stage. He will swing from one end of the spectrum to the other. His insecurity will present as silence, brooding, and sullenness in one moment and being irritable, volatile, and argumentative in the next.

We won't always be able to predict the extremes, but we can certainly be aware of what is happening with him, and much like our toddler boys needed help, he'll need assistance in turning the insecurity (and all that comes with it) into something constructive. He'll need a safe place to take the emotion, as well as outlets to feel his strength and to feel purpose. He will be extreme in his words. When he does speak, he's vulnerable to saying things like: "You *always* make me . . ." "You *never* let me . . ." "You are the *only* parent who . . ."

We'll spend a great amount of time saying "try again" to him in this stage. He will need to rephrase, rework, rethink, retry, and redeem his words and responses throughout this stage. He will be consumed with himself one moment and completely unaware of himself in another. It will seem puzzling that a young man who is so acutely aware of how he looks can be so clueless about how harsh he just sounded.

As he hits the mark and (more often) misses the mark, he will need mercy and understanding. You will never have as great an opportunity to reflect the mercy of our God to your son as you will in parenting an adolescent boy. You will have the opportunity to live out the truth of His mercies being new every morning. Your son will need you to extend new mercy to him each day as he is stumbling, struggling, and steadying himself in his adolescence. It's a bumpy stretch of the road. As much pushing away, separating out, and individuating as is taking place, it would be easy to leave him to himself much of the time, but he desperately needs your input, involvement, and investment. (I will make some suggestions on how to do this in the "Try it Out" section.)

Read the chapter in *Wild Things* on "Ceremonies and Rites of Passage." Consider celebrating your son and calling out who God is making him to be.

Reassess his outlets for testing his strength and mind, and experiencing risk, adventure, and purpose.

Reread the story of the prodigal son and how a young man who wandered was received following a mistake.

Share these suggestions for parents of daughters:

Read the section in *Raising Girls* on "The Autonomous Years." How do you see your daughter emerging from the narcissistic years?

Where do you see her confidence?

Where do you see her questioning herself?

What do you like about your daughter?

How could you help her see those things in herself?

What are three strengths you see in her that you could tell her about today?

In the last stage of their development, we want to help girls find their place in the world. "Want to help" is the operative phrase here. As parents, as adults who love these girls, we can no longer do it for them. Most often, they are making the choices now. We can't choose their friends any longer. We can't shelter them and keep them away from all potentially dangerous situations. We actually never could. But what we can do in these important, autonomous years is help.

You can point out the characteristics and strengths that God is growing inside of your daughter. She is great with people, an amazing artist, and so forth. You can give her room to make mistakes and then help her pick up the pieces, or give her consequences when need be. With every year, she needs more freedom and more privileges. You can offer opportunities for her to connect and relate in ways that bring life and hope. Make volunteering mandatory, but give her options as to where she volunteers so that she can actually experience making a difference. You can help her gain confidence in herself and your readiness for her to leave home and enter the world.

Your daughter is becoming her own person in these years. Just last week, I sat with a senior in high school named Lizzie who talked about how she was ready to move on to college and make new friends who really liked her. My response was that what mattered the most right now is that she liked herself. Lizzie's response was, "I think I actually do . . . or at least I do some of the time." Some of the time is honestly good enough in the life of a girl—at least this side of heaven. It is something to pray for in every stage of your daughter's life, but maybe particularly in this one.

How would your daughter answer that question? It might be worth asking. And it is more than worth an opportunity for her to use her voice to begin to name the gifts God has placed inside of her. Then, it's your turn to have the honor of agreeing. In this stage of her life, you want her to find her voice, to gain confidence, to like herself, to have healthy, supportive relationships, and to develop her own sense of intimacy with a God who likes and loves her far more than she could imagine—all of the time.

Parent Perspective

"I've figured out what's wrong with all of the kids I know and their relationships with their parents," a high school senior said after school one day to her mom.

"Really. I'd love to know what you think the problem is," her mom said with amused interest.

"Their parents are trying to make the kids into who they think they should be rather than who they are."

Hmmmm. Does that statement stir anything inside of you? Frustration? Irritation? Even a little fear? A father once said in my counseling office, "I've realized that all of the things I don't like in my son are the very things I don't like about myself."

Children and parents. This stage in a child's life, for a boy, is largely about extricating himself from his parents. For a girl, it is about discovering herself on her own. Both have to do with you. Both have to do with separation. And separation is never easy.

Often, as you are raising your children, it's hard to know where they end and you begin. From the very earliest stages of his life, you sleep when he sleeps and wake up when he cries in the night. You hurt when he hurts, emotionally and even sometimes, physically. You are her caretaker, provider, hero, and often her best friend. Weeping with those who weep and rejoicing with those who rejoice feel like second nature as a parent of children in stages 1-3.

Then adolescence hits—and hits hard. You have been all of these things and more to your son and your daughter. And, in some ways, they have become an extension of you. Your identities are so closely linked as parent and child that sometimes they're indistinguishable. But now, you have hit a stage where, in order for your son and daughter to continue to mature, they have to be distinguished. They have to separate. You have to let go. Ouch.

Lead parents to share aloud three strengths in their sons or daughters.

Challenge: Pick one strength and write a note this week to your son or daughter and leave it somewhere for them to find.

Lead each parent to talk about their adolescence and if they felt pressure (spoken or unspoken) to be or do something specific from their parents.

Do any of them see themselves leaning in the same direction? If so, ask them if they'd be willing to share.

It is my experience that moms, in these years, are often harder on their daughters and fathers are harder on their sons. I have spoken to several mothers whose daughters have chosen a career path that is "just not an option." The way their daughters dress, their manner of relating, and their commitment to detail are different from their mother's—and therefore not OK

For dads, it is often a lack of common interests. Boys who won't play sports, who aren't as motivated academically, who aren't dating as much as their fathers did. These boys have an ability to embarrass their dads that seems to be more about the dads than it really is about the sons.

I was teaching a parenting class recently and a very sweet mother came up to me and said, "I'm afraid I'm being overly critical of my daughter. She is just so different than I was or even am. I was quiet as a little girl, where she's loud. I was always on the outside. She likes to be the center of attention. I don't want to squash her. But I can't seem to find the line between being critical and helping her grow."

That line is hard to find . . . for every one of us. Your daughter may remind you of yourself when she was your age. Or your son may be completely different. Her weaknesses bother you because you struggle in the same ways. He frustrates you because he is just so different from what you were. And you thought he would want to follow in your footsteps.

My hope for you, the hope of all three of us, is that you would be committed to praying for God's plan for your son or daughter's life. His plan may be different from yours. Actually, His plan will probably be different from yours. It will involve smiley faces, rejoicing, and some failures along the way, too. But your son's failures are your son's failures. Not yours. Your daughter will make choices that are entirely different from those you would make yourself or even those you would make for her. They're her choices as she moves into adulthood. Keep praying. Pray that God would continue to reveal His will, His plan. Your job as a parent, and especially a stage 4 parent, is to help your child become who God has created them to be. Your job is to help. Their job is to become. And God's job—His wise, perfect, omnipotent job—is to come up with the plan.

~TRY IT OUT~
For Parents of Girls

Especially in these years, girls are either being introduced or about to be introduced to a plethora of outside influences—*influences* really being too subtle of a word. *Pressure,* or even *demands,* does more to describe the force they will feel of the world pushing in on them. However, for some kids, it will be more of a pull than a push. And that pull has a great deal of mystery and allure.

You can no longer protect your daughter when she leaves the safety of your roof. But you can be very strategic in gradually giving her a taste of what's to come. And that taste can help ward off the force and the allure.

This is where that idea of "increasing by increments" comes in. You want to be very strategic in these last few years of your daughter's development. We really believe it's important to come up with a game plan today—no matter how old your daughter is. Think about her bedtime if she's younger, her curfew if she's older. Think about the movies you allow her to watch and privileges she has access to from a technological standpoint. Each of those freedoms needs to be increasing with every year. You want her boundaries to widen gradually for two reasons:

1) Your daughter will mess up. And you'd much rather her mess up when she's living in the safety of home. You can help pick up the pieces and offer consequences when called for. You live in the balance between letting the rope out and pulling it right back in when she's gone too far.

2) You want the differences in her freedoms to be barely noticeable when she leaves home. That can prevent, as we said in the video, the "Woo hoo! Free at last!" phenomenon that so many kids experience in college.

Teenagers want control. Girls especially do in these final teenage years. And the more we choose our battles and give

Extra ideas for sons:

Choose some movies to watch with your son that open the door to some good conversations about life and relationships. A few ideas would be:

October Sky

Radio

Remember the Titans

The Count of Monte Cristo

Simon Birch

Dead Poets Society

My Dog Skip

Lord of the Flies

Empire of the Sun

Identify a family that you enjoy, that shares your values, and that has a son your son's age. Sign up together to build a Habitat for Humanity house, serve in a soup kitchen, go on a short term missions trip, or volunteer to serve at a camp for inner-city kids. He needs the outlet to feel purpose and will likely enjoy the experience differently with a friend.

Choose a book to read with him about his journey to become a man. Read a chapter a week and go to a local donut or coffee shop to have a conversation with him about it. Consider partnering with some other fathers and sons to experience this.

them control in small, safe doses, the less they'll push for it in reckless ways.

The complaints I probably hear the most are from the girls who are making wise, good (at least in terms of major teenager issues) choices. They're not drinking, using drugs, sneaking out, or sleeping with their boyfriends. Their comments to me are, "I'm a good kid and I have no idea why my parents won't trust me. It's not fair when the wild kids are the ones who are getting to stay out late." And, honestly, I agree.

If your daughter has worked hard to earn your trust, give it to her. If she acts responsibly and makes good choices, reward her with your trust. Not "Sure, stay out all night" kind of trust. But stretch the limits of your comfort zone. I believe that girls still, in these years, really want to please you. They will often rise to the level of trust you place in them. And, the more you give, the more leverage you have when you pull it back, if she gets in trouble.

Give them roots and wings, as they say. You have given her roots for so many years, in the truths you have taught and the ways you have loved and delighted in her. Now, is when you have an opportunity to help her try out those wings.

~TRY IT OUT~
For Parents of Boys

As Melissa mentioned, we are all three training puppies. If you walked into the Daystar office, you'd be tempted to say that Melissa and Sissy are succeeding at this task, and you'd struggle to say something positive about my efforts in this category.

Every Saturday, I pile my children and Owen into the car and we head to Puppy School. At the last class, while the other dogs were heeling, sitting, lying in a down position, and staying for extended periods of time, Owen was growling, wandering around my legs and tangling us both in a web of leash. Every time I gave the command he'd look at me grumpily, half-follow through, make this grumbling, growling sound and reach for the treat. The teacher walked over to Owen and said, "feeling a little snarky, are we?" She was spot on with that word. It well described Owen and a number of other snarky creatures I spend time with regularly.

I went home and looked up the definition of "snarky" and found everything from snide and sarcastic, to testy and irritable, growly and reactive. I even ran across a dog trainer/vet in Connecticut offering "Snarky Dog Classes." They advertise the class for "dogs who act inappropriately in public. They may react to people, dogs, or distractions in general. The goal of the Snarky Dog class is to help you better read your dog to prevent the inappropriate behavior, and to teach and encourage your dog to do the right thing."

I think adolescent boys are snarky. They are snide and sarcastic, testy and irritable, growly and reactive. I'm thinking of offering a class titled "Snarky Teenage Boys." I could borrow their description. "This class is for boys who act inappropriately in public or at home. They may react to people and get distracted. The goal is to help you better understand your son to prevent the inappropriate behavior and to teach your son to do the right thing."

The truth is that our snarky boys do need us to understand them better. They need us to take a deeper look at the biological chaos that plagues them, the arrogance and insecurity, why he's so argumentative and his need to individuate. This snarky young man needs other voices, mercy and forgiveness, and the outlets we've discussed.

We train snarky dogs with treats and affirmation. A snarky teenage boy loves food and needs a lot of affirmation as well. Work hard to catch him in some good moments. Release him to other trusted, positive, adult voices. Adolescent boys have an ability to hear from them differently.

Plan a day trip or weekend trip to a place he'd love. Camp, hike, fish, travel to an out-of-town stadium for a game, find a band he loves on tour and go to that city, search for the world's fastest roller-coasters, try out a water park. Choose an opportunity to spend time with him with the primary focus being enjoyment rather than instruction.

For early adolescent boys, I'd recommend:

Flight Plan: Your Mission to Become a Man by Lee Burns and Braxton Brady

Do Hard Things: A Teenage Rebellion Against Low Expectations by Alex and Brett Harris

For mid to late adolescent boys, I'd recommend:

Wild at Heart by John Eldredge

How to Hit a Curveball, Grill the Perfect Steak and Become a Real Man by Stephen James and David Thomas

Daily Conversations

Driving Toward Confidence

"For you have been my hope, O Sovereign Lord, my confidence since my youth." –Psalm 71:5, NIV

Do you remember the first time you got behind a wheel? For both boys and girls, this stage is when they learn to drive (unless you live in one of the crazier states where they let narcissistic-age girls and boys behind the wheel). But, for most kids, they will find themselves in these years, sitting beside you. Heart racing, palms sweaty . . . and we haven't even started talking about them yet.

Instilling confidence is one of the chapters Sissy and I included in our book, *Modern Parents, Vintage Values*. In these years, your child feels anything but confident. It's funny how many teenagers will tell me their favorite verse is Philippians 4:13—*I can do all things through Christ who strengthens me*. I think that's for a reason. I think guys and girls cling to this verse as an answer to their insecurity . . . as hope for who they can be.

Driving is just one way that they have an opportunity to move away from you and toward their own identity, their own sense of confidence. You will be terrified they'll make mistakes—fail—wreck themselves and their cars. And, quite possibly, they will. It will be hard for you to watch. But they need the experience of living, which includes the experience of making mistakes.

For your son to learn to walk, you had to stand at a distance and let him walk toward—or away from you. He would toddle a few steps and then fall flat on his bottom. You were his safety net to explore the world. You are still that safety net today. Now, instead of toddling away, he's driving. He is driving toward becoming a confident man. She is driving toward a confidence in who she is and what she has to offer. But we've got to let them drive. They can do all things with Christ who strengthens them. And so can you—including letting them back down your driveway.

The Power of Encouragement

"For you know that we dealt with each of you as a father deals with his own children, encouraging, comforting and urging you to live lives worthy of God, who calls you into his kingdom and glory."
–1 Thessalonians 2:11-12, NIV

Every year, we have a fundraiser called "The Bike Thing." Several years ago, I remember riding behind a 17-year-old girl and her dad. The last few miles had proved to be a challenge. They were on these little, irritating, laborious hills. She was bent over the handle bars of her bike, pedaling hard. Her dad must have seen the effort it was taking her at the end. He quietly rode up beside her, put his hand on her back, and pushed. I think he pushed her all of the way to the finish line, or at least until the people standing at the finish line would have seen his hand on her back. Then he let her cross on her own.

When I think about 1 Thessalonians 2:11-12, I think the easiest parts to master in parenting teenagers are the urging and comforting. But it's so often the encouragement they need the most in these years. And the kind of encouragement they need is no longer the running in front of them and shouting "You can do it!" as they learn to ride their bike that we did in their younger years. It's the quietly riding up beside them and placing our hand on their back. And then removing it just in time for them to feel like they are the ones who really can do it.

You have an opportunity to encourage them, to answer their questions, speak to their fears—even when they are unspoken. The trick with teenagers is answering them in a way where you offer just enough encouragement to encourage, but not so much that they feel like they've done it because of your encouragement.

Keep urging and comforting, but don't forget the power of encouragement. It doesn't take a lot, but just enough to get them past those last few years—and hills—of their development.

How could you encourage your son today? Where does your daughter need your support? How can you come alongside him or her in a way that helps him or her feel like you're there, but he or she is the one who can do it?

Food Fights

"So if the Son sets you free, you will be free indeed." –John 8:36, NIV

"Food and I just don't get along," a high school girl said to me a few years back. Let me say right here . . . I am not the healthiest eater. If I were marooned on a desert island, the food I would most want to have with me would be queso and chips. And, honestly, I have no clue which kind of fat is in queso—but I do know enough to know that it's probably not a good kind. I think this is in part because I'm a little rebellious. It's not that I don't care about my body. I just have been around too many people who care too much. Another teenager said to me, "I have given myself over to this god of thinness." I feel strongly that our bodies and diets have taken on entirely too much importance in our culture, much to the detriment of young girls.

I know very healthy—physically and emotionally—vegetarians who change their diets because of animal cruelty. I applaud these folks who are much more disciplined than my queso-eating self. But I worry about girls. I particularly worry about girls and our love/hate relationship with food. And if there's ever an age that it kicks in, it's this one. They want more control over their lives. They are expecting a lot out of themselves. And, as we said in the video, their hormones slow down after puberty and cause them to become curvier.

In the video, we said, "If you have issues with food, your daughter most likely will, too." In *The Back Door to Your Teen's Heart,* we talked about those crazy fun house mirrors. We look in them and see ourselves as taller or shorter or fatter than we really are. You are a mirror for your daughter's growing identity. You hold it up to her herself. And when your image is distorted, you will reflect a distorted image right back to her.

I have walked with countless women who have struggled with eating issues. You can be free. With Jesus and the wise counsel of a trusted friend and/or professional as your guides, you can experience a freedom from this love/hate relationship with food. You can live life confident that you are much more than the sum of your body parts. God has given you a hope and a future that doesn't have to be defined by the way you look . . . and might include a little queso.

Dignity and Respect

"Fathers, do not embitter your children, or they will become discouraged." –Colossians 3:21, NIV

I (David) met with a family this week that moved from out of state when the father's company transferred him. The move has been difficult for everyone, particularly their 16-year-old son. He liked his old school, his old friends, his old house, and according to him "everything about my old life." He has become more sullen, withdrawn, and in turn, depressed.

At an honest point in the conversation, the boy admitted to withholding to punish his parents for the move. He knew they were concerned and wanting information about his life. He felt their desperation and said "conversations with the two of you start to feel like an interrogation by the Counter-Terrorist Unit. Sometimes I just don't want to talk, especially when you force me to do it."

I asked the parents what they were hearing and how they wanted to respond. The mom offered to give him some space, permission to say he didn't want to talk, and a chance to negotiate a time to talk at some later point. The boy looked mildly relieved. The father moved up to the edge of his seat, pointed his finger at me and exclaimed, "Not you or any other yahoo is gonna tell me when I can and can't ask my son questions. I don't need permission to be a parent. I'll ask questions when I want answers, and it doesn't concern me whether it's good timing for him or not."

I said, "There's no dignity in demanding someone speak to you on your terms. So you can keep trying to force him to talk to you if that makes you feel more in control, or you can try something more honoring to your son who is struggling."

Fortunately, he backed down a step. It created enough space for him to look at his son—to look through this boy's anger and resistance to see his hurt and his ache. This family has a long way to go, but they took some small steps in the right direction that day.

As you require respect with your children, are you equally focused on parenting them with respect and dignity?

Designed for the Job at Hand

"Are you tired? Worn out? Burned out on religion? Come to me. Get away with me and you'll recover your life. I'll show you how to take a real rest. Walk with me and work with me—watch how I do it. Learn the unforced rhythms of grace. I won't lay anything heavy or ill-fitting on you. Keep company with me and you'll learn to live freely and lightly." –Matthew 11:28-30, The Message

I (David) love these words. I need these words. I forget these words. I've read them more times than I could count, and I need to hear them again and again. I live more days than I care to admit as if I've never heard these words before. I know the place to go with my weariness, my anxiety, and my fear. And yet I live like I've no clue what to do.

I reread those words a couple of years ago and began reconsidering the words "I won't lay anything heavy or ill-fitting on you." I started thinking about all the things that burden me, how much I carry, and all the things I fear and hold on to.

I think about moments in my own journey of parenting when I've lost sleep over something taking place with one of my children—their health, their struggles, their relationships. I worry about my role in it—am I doing enough or am I doing too much? I worry about the outcome—how will this affect them in the short and long term? I worry if they have enough resilience to make their way through a particular challenge or struggle?

There are moments where it just feels like too much—more than I am capable of handling. Then I remember this promise. Nothing I'm given in my journey will be too heavy or ill-fitting. There are plenty of challenges that exist within my parenting that feel better suited for someone else, but the reality is that it all fits on me. As Melissa said earlier, I'm designed to be the father to my three children. And you are designed to be the parent to yours. That was written before time began. Nothing we come up against in our journey of parenting is ill-fitting. It may feel that way in many moments, but it's exactly as God intended it to be.

Where are some particular areas of parenting that feel ill-fitting right now? Is there a particular struggle you are carrying that may cause you to parent more out of fear than out of love?

Keeping Your Eye on the Path

"Finally, brothers, whatever is true, whatever is noble, whatever is right, whatever is pure, whatever is lovely, whatever is admirable—if anything is excellent or praiseworthy—think about such things."
-Philippians 4:8, NIV

Sissy and I went mountain-biking a few years back with our friend Pace. None of the three of us had ever been mountain biking. But how hard could it be? You ride up the ski lift and have those wide, green, ski runs to come down. This is not the way it works—at all. They drive you up this windy mountain and put you on the "back side" of the ski area. No green slopes in sight. When the man dropped us off, his last words were "Don't worry about the obstacles. Just focus on the path and you'll do fine."

Obstacles. The obstacles on our path were trees and big boulder-type rocks. I hit most of them on the way down. I would start going and think "Don't look at the rock, don't look at the rock" and Bam! I'd hit the rock. "Forget about the tree, forget about the tree, Melissa" and soon I'd have pine needles sticking out of my socks. Sissy and Pace laughed that every time I caught up to them (stopped and waiting) I'd have a new trickle of blood running down my leg.

Toward the end, however, I learned to focus on the path. When I kept my eyes fixed on where I was going, rather than the obstacles around me, my ride was actually easier—with much fewer bumps and accidents along the way.

There are a whole lot of obstacles in these last few years of raising your boys and girls. There are cars and boys, drama and girls, being invited to parties, not being invited to parties, arguing, power struggles, breakups, heartaches, and a whole host of other hiccups your children will hit in these years. You could be swallowed up in fear if you focus too long. But Paul, in his letter to the Philippians, said his version of "focus on the path." And we would echo his words to you.

Think about what is excellent in your son. Tell your daughter what is praiseworthy about her. Give thanks for the true and right and pure things about your child. We promise they are there. God has placed so much good inside your son and your daughter, even in these autonomous and wandering years. Think about such things.

A Day of Rest

"Oh! May the God of green hope fill you up with joy, fill you up with peace, so that your believing lives, filled with the life-giving energy of the Holy Spirit, will brim over with hope!" –Romans 15:13, The Message

We want you to take this day as a day of rest. Our prayer, today, is that you will find rest and refreshment through Christ. You are in the place He has chosen you to be. God is a God of hope, joy, and peace. May He grant you that today and this week in your journey to raising boys and girls.

Notes:

A FINAL NOTE

Parent out of love and not out of fear.

Parenting is a stirring journey. With all of the information you've received about your son's or daughter's development, you could easily be stirred to fear. But our hope is that this material has stirred you to something much more . . .

If we could leave you with anything, at the end of this series, it would be a sense of hope. You have been chosen. God has specifically called you to be the parent of your child. What matters most, in the midst of all the "he is . . ." and "he needs . . ." and "she is . . ." and "she needs . . ." is not that you cross every one of those items off the list. It's the quality of relationship you offer your son or daughter. It's that you're you while you're helping him become him or her become her. You're not going to get it right, at times. You will fail. But we serve a God who redeems. He redeems every failure you have had or will have as a parent. His gracious love takes the place of fear. And that is enough to hang your hope on. You can raise your boys and girls out of love, not fear, through and because of Jesus.

Listening Guide

Icebreaker—
Have each
person say
"I would like
to thank this
group for
_____."

With _____, you are _____ out

who God has _____ your _____ to be.

Ingredients of naming:

1. _____—Enjoyment of who _____

are and who _____ are

2. _____ with your own _____

3. _____—We celebrate them when they

_____ and when they _____

You cannot directly _____ the

_____ of a child.

The quality of _____ is what lasts.

There is a healthy _____ and _____

of what's going on.

But the fear can begin to _____ us.

Confidence comes from a combination of _____

and _____.

Parent out of _____ and not out of

_____.

Parenting out of love is being willing to _____

yourself.

Don't lose _____.

God's perfect _____ casts out _____.

Ask the participants the following questions:

What was one fear you had at the beginning of this series?

What is one area about which you could echo the words of the mom Melissa overheard on the phone, "Our son's normal!"?

If you wanted to remember one concept from the teaching, what would it be?

Summary

When David, Sissy and I teach, I usually let them go first. They have these great things to offer, such as all of the specific things I can't ever remember. I couldn't even begin to talk about technology or consequences or any of the practical things they speak to so well. But, what I love to do, as they're talking, is watch you. As a matter of fact, I wish I could have been sitting off to the side watching as you watched this video. The facial expressions of moms and dads in our audiences are always so telling. There are always the smiles of "We've got that one down!" the chuckles of "That's my boy," the wide eyes of "Do girls really start their periods that young?" the small catches of breath with "Whoops, I already read his journal!" and so on. You get the picture.

Sissy and my newest book is called *Modern Parents, Vintage Values*. In it, we talk a lot about those practical things. Sissy wrote a lot of those sections. My favorite part is the end. It's actually the last 13 pages of a 262-page book. A friend of ours recently called after reading it and said, "Well I don't know what I would have done without those last few pages. As I read the first three-fourths of the book, all I did was panic over all of the things I haven't known and definitely haven't done! The end was the part that gave me hope."

Parenting out of fear. It's the most natural response in the world. There is so much to know and do. Those are David's and Sissy's parts. My part is to give you hope.

Do you remember that question—"Would you tell us the secret to making sure our child grows up Christ-centered and well-rounded?" And do you remember my answer, "No. Let's just keep it a secret." It's not that it's a secret. It's that it is not possible. You can not make sure your child grows up Christ-centered and well-rounded. You can not make them happy or godly or selfless, either. You can not directly change the heart of a child. My hope is that knowing that fact takes away some of your fear.

You may be the parent who's afraid that you can't do it right. You live with a tightness inside that makes it difficult at times to enjoy your child. My answer to you is that you can't do it right. But that knowledge can free you to love. What matters the most is not your performance as a parent, but your desire to be a godly parent. And what you can do is apologize, ask for forgiveness, and forgive him or her when he fails.

You may be the parent who is afraid of losing relationship. You don't discipline because you want him to like you . . . you want her to keep talking to you. For you, I want you to know that it may look like you lose your relationship temporarily. But nothing and no one takes away the fact that you are your child's mom or dad. He feels safe when you offer boundaries. She needs you to hold her hand and point your finger. Be bigger and stronger than your child. He already has buddies. What he needs is a strong, loving parent.

It may be that you're the parent who has a hard time trusting your son or daughter after he or she has failed. He betrayed your trust. How can you still believe in who she can be when you don't really like who she is? God can give you a vision for your child that stretches way beyond your own. He has that kind of vision for me . . . and for you. Pray that he will give you that kind of belief in your child. Your child needs you to believe in him or her, because he most likely doesn't believe in himself.

Or you may be the parent who thinks "Nothing works. I've tried all of these things already," and so you throw up your hands. To you, I would say, "Stay close. Stay engaged. And stay consistent." It is humbling to stay involved when your child is not responding. But he needs your presence. She needs to know that you care, and throwing up your hands feels like giving up to her. In those times, she's often already given up on herself.

You can not directly change the heart of your child. At times, you will want to—desperately. He will disappoint you. She will hurt you. As Proverbs 17:25 says, a foolish son brings grief to his father and bitterness to his mother. Your child will make foolish choices. And, again, the most natural response in those times is fear.

Make the following suggestions:

Plan a time with your son or daughter that is solely about enjoyment and not instruction.

Pick a birthday coming up for your child and plan a celebration. Involve important voices in his or her life.

Ask the following questions:

What are you afraid of right now for your son or daughter?

What are you afraid of for yourself, as a parent?

How are you trying hard and missing out on enjoying your son or daughter?

What does it look like for you to parent out of love?

How can you entrust your child to God?

Choose a verse that reflects a theme right now in your parenting, and can remind you not to lose heart.

There are more than 300 verses in the Bible about fear. But fear locks you in the present, where you miss the big picture. The big picture takes us back to 2 Timothy 1:12. He is able to protect what you entrust to him. Confidence is a combination of hope and trust. You can have confidence in Him, even when you don't have confidence in your son or daughter—or in your own parenting.

He is able. He is the reason you can parent out of love and not out of fear. And, in response to all of those verses about fear, He says "Don't lose heart." The heart He is talking about is you . . . your personality. Don't lose yourself in the midst of trying to get it all right. It is the quality of relationship that matters. David and Sissy will talk more about what that quality looks like in their "Try It Out" sections.

But, for now, I want to leave you with hope. I want to leave you with the hope that is ours in Christ. He is the perfect parent—our perfect Father. He has called you and He is able to keep that which you have entrusted to Him. Don't lose heart.

Parent Perspective

We all have a fear of unpredictability and uncertainty. In other words, a fear of not knowing what's happening now or what's about to happen. And if there's ever anything that's unpredictable and uncertain, it's parenting.

How many times have you wondered what your son is really up to? How many times have you been afraid for your daughter to go to school, not knowing if she'll fail another test, be hurt by another friend, make the basketball team, and a million other unpredictable variables? The not knowing . . . it's what so often gets you, as a parent.

But there are other factors that sometimes make the unpredictability and uncertainty even scarier . . . to be more specific, two other factors that are roughly the size of an almond. Deep within the temporal lobe of your brain are two structures called amygdalae (amygdala, in their singular form). The amygdala has a lot to do with fear. For example, when something frightens you, messages are sent via your neural pathways to your amygdala, which determines the seriousness of the situation and then determines a fight or flight response.

Another function of your amygdala is that it stores memories, particularly memories of strong emotion. And the amazing thing is that the amygdala's memory is so strong that it doesn't just house the memory of a fearful event; it houses the feelings that came with it.

That's probably enough of a science lesson for now. But, all of this goes to say that sometimes our reactions or our fears are stronger based on our own memories. You put your own memories of fear along with fear and anxiety about the future with the unpredictability and uncertainty of being a parent, and your amygdala is working overtime. It's no wonder our natural response is to parent out of fear, and that fear creates such a tightness in us.

We have talked a lot about what it looks like to parent out of love, to have confidence in God and His love for both you and your child. But what do you do with the fear? When your daughter has to have surgery, when you can't reach your son on his new cell phone, when your daughter still isn't home 45 minutes after curfew, when the arguing just continues, when he can't seem to get his grades up, and a million other daily events happen in your parenting journey, fear is a very real and present companion. So, what do you do with it?

1) Name it. So often, parents isolate themselves because of a fear of judgment. It's hard to talk honestly to other parents who aren't talking honestly. Every parent you know feels fear. Every parent you know has some type of worry for and with their child. You are not alone and are not meant to be alone in this journey. Talk to your spouse and/or a group of friends. Find a safe place to bring your fear out into the open. If fear stays inside of you, it will grow. Bring it out into the light—into the light of a community of like-minded believers who can encourage and help calm you.

Go back to Melissa's statement, "God has chosen you to be the parent of _____." Why do you think God chose you specifically?

Lead each parent to name one strength they bring to the table to offer their child.

Ask the following questions to parents of girls:

What is the version of your daughter you have been reflecting to her?

What are three positive character-istics you see in her?

Read Chapter 13 in *Raising Girls*. How could you name your daughter today?

How could you enjoy her for who she is right now?

How is God prompting you to look at your life, with this study?

What type of celebration/rite of passage could you plan for a big birthday coming up?

2) Step outside of your world. Your fears as a parent can become all-consuming if you don't give yourself breaks. Work in your garden. Take an art class. Play golf. Go for a run. Eat dinner out with your spouse or a friend. Go see a movie. It's easy to get so focused on your children that you don't have anything bringing you alive as a person, apart from the kids. You and they need you to have outside interests, to be a person and not just a parent.

Scientists say that the amygdala responds to calm words and presence. It's hard to find either, on a good morning, when you're trying to get three children fed, homework in their backpacks, and into the car to get to school on time. Throw in a few everyday fearful events, like tests or friendship troubles, and then add a divorce or other type of trauma in your family. This is honestly normal life for most of us. Unpredictability and uncertainty. And, all of a sudden, you've found yourself accustomed to living in the chaos and the fear.

You don't have to. Calm words and presence can calm not only the amygdala, but also the chaos surrounding your home.

"God wants the combination of his steady, constant calling and warm, personal counsel in Scripture to come to characterize us, keeping us alert for whatever he will do next." –Romans 15:4b, The Message

"Keeping us alert for whatever He will do next" implies a confidence that whatever He will do will be for our good. Confidence, remember, is trust and hope combined. He wants the combination of His steady, constant calling and warm, personal counsel to come to characterize us. Sounds a lot like calm words and presence to me.

You will have fears, as a parent. Your life will be unpredictable and uncertain at times, as will the life of your child. But you can be alert without being afraid, looking forward to whatever good he will do next—for you and your family.

"May our dependably steady and warmly personal God develop maturity in you so that you get along with each other as well as Jesus gets along with us all. Then we'll be a choir—not our voices only, but our very lives singing in harmony in a stunning anthem to the God and Father of our Master Jesus!" –Romans 15:5-6, The Message

RAISING BOYS AND GIRLS

~TRY IT OUT~
For Parents of Girls

What are three ways you could name her in this stage of her life? (For example, tell her what you admire in her, write her a note, find a verse that reminds you of her, paint her a picture, etc.)

More than anyone else in these first 19 years of your daughter's life, you speak to the truth of who she is. You hold up that mirror we talked about—help her see not only who she is today, but who she's becoming. Would you want her to expect the future men in her life to make her feel the same way you have? Would you want the version of herself you have shown her to be the version she believes?

Naming is a profoundly important job. Revelation 2:17 points to the name Jesus will give us when we get to heaven. Throughout Scripture, naming was used to define and redefine God's chosen people . . . Jacob to Israel, Simon to "Rock," Saul to Paul. Those names speak to God's calling on the life of the one named.

You obviously are not going to know what God has called your daughter to do when she's 2 or 12, but you will have glimpses into who He has called her to be. Speak to those glimpses. Help her see herself as you see her. Point out the characteristics you enjoy and respect in her. Name her in the way that only her mom or dad can. Part of how naming takes place include the three ideas we talked about in the video: enjoyment, dealing with your own stuff, and celebration.

In the first stage in a girl's life, we said that girls who are delighted in feel more delightful. This takes place over the course of her entire life. Just by enjoying her, you help her gain more confidence. By enjoyment, we mean spending time with her when you are not teaching, instructing, or correcting her in any way. The purpose of your time together is to enjoy each other. Play a game. Go for a walk. Watch her favorite cartoon. If she's older, watch the early seasons of "The Gilmore Girls" together. Do something she loves—or show her something you love.

Make the following suggestions to parents of boys:

Consider writing a mission statement for your son. Define who you hope him to be as an adult man. Let those words create a framework for your parenting journey. How do those ideas align with how you currently spend your days and weeks as a family? How would you want to begin adjusting your commitments and your current involvement as a family to be more congruent with who you hope he becomes as an adult man?

Choose a moment to interview your son about yourself. Ask him to list three of your

The dealing with your own stuff is the least enjoyable part of naming. How different would your life be today if your parents had been willing to look at theirs? Your willingness to acknowledge your stuff—your failures, your sin—can help her not only respect you more as she grows up, but it can give her a deeper understanding of her own need for Christ. And it can help you to be a better—and freer—parent.

I talk with too many girls who are afraid of growing up. They are terrified of the changes in their bodies and emotions. Those who have older siblings are often terrified of the changes that will take place in their relationships with you. She needs to know that becoming a woman is something to be celebrated. Girls are so critical of themselves, as are women. For her to look forward to puberty, to see becoming a woman as a gift, can help ward off just a little of the self-hatred she will battle as a female.

Your daughter is a gift. She is a mixture of sugar and spice and everything nice, with a little adolescent drama thrown in for a few years. She will look to you, in different ways, at different times, to help her understand herself. You are her first and most influential teacher in terms of who she is, what she has to offer, and how Jesus loves her. You name her first—and continue to name her for the rest of her life in the way you enjoy her, celebrate her, and speak the truth of who God has uniquely, beautifully made her to be.

~TRY IT OUT~
For Parents of Boys

Over the years, we've had the luxury of playing soccer with several families that are friends. Our friends, Sean and Betsy, have a son named Michael, who is one of those boys who was born a gifted athlete. He is the kind of kid whom you could throw about any kind of ball at and he would instinctively take to the sport. I commented to his mom that it won't be long before their phone starts ringing with men interested in recruiting this gifted young athlete. She commented that it had already started. Betsy shut down the recruiting operation by saying, "He has a coach right now who pulls him off the field when he isn't passing the ball, and I love everything about that." Betsy understands that left to his own devices (or in the hands of an uber-competitive, winning-obsessed father/coach), her son could evolve into a ball hog, a boy who is more committed to his own performance than anything. I reminded my friend that she is a rare breed. She is wisely committed to nurturing character in her son. Are we invested in the things that matter for the boys we love? Are we willing to make the needed sacrifices throughout his development to create opportunity for him to encounter struggle, sacrifice, and service? Are we more committed to his happiness or his becoming responsible?

He needs us to maintain a big picture perspective on parenting. We want to consistently be thinking about who he is becoming and parenting forward. If we only parent with today in mind, we can over-commit to his current happiness rather than consider his future benefit. I often challenge moms to consider that they may one day have a daughter-in-law. Will that relationship be one of gratitude or resentment? You'd like your daughter-in-law to be thinking more about what a great man you raised than what an irresponsible, emotionally immature, attention-seeking, over-sized boy her husband is.

The commitment to our boys continues as we look closely at ourselves. We are watching for where our baggage spills over into him. We have a life that communicates we are people first and parents second. When we live from that place, we can spill joy, contentment, and hope into him. Remember that having life outside of our sons doesn't communicate disinterest but rather contentment. It also takes an enormous burden off our kids emotionally. They don't feel responsible for our happiness.

We are enough and we aren't enough. You are exactly who God had in mind for your son and He has equipped you for the task at hand. You aren't enough and never will be. The truth is that you have everything you need through Jesus. He has equipped you to parent your son individually and He is available to meet your needs.

closest friends, three of your hobbies/interests/passions, and how you'd choose to spend an available Saturday morning. Listen to see how aware he is of your life outside of him.

Identify three individuals who will tell you the truth about yourself as a person and a parent. Ask them to give you some honest feedback about what they observe. Invite them to be as truthful as possible as a means of growing as an individual and as a parent.

Daily Conversations

Loving Your Children Well

"Not only so, but we also rejoice in our sufferings, because we know that suffering produces perseverance; perseverance, character; and character, hope. And hope does not disappoint us, because God has poured out his love into our hearts by the Holy Spirit, whom he has given us." –Romans 5:3-5

"Loving someone well" is a phrase that bounces around in our community a lot. I can't love anybody well for long. I would imagine you can't either. How well do you love your son when you're on your 13th night in a row of four hours of sleep? How well do you love your daughter when she learns the word "No!" and says it 27 times per hour? Or when your son spills Coke on your brand new couch? Or a million other scenarios that will present themselves over the course of your parenting? When these times come up, I'm not even sure loving well is the issue at hand.

I was preparing for a talk on this very subject and asked a group of high school girls if they thought their parents had loved them well. One girl looked at me, raised her shoulders, and said "ish?" "Ish" is right. Or we could say from time to time.

This side of heaven, our loving well is going to be ish-ish. It's going to come in glimpses. You'll love your children wonderfully, and then you'll fail them. You'll say powerful, life-giving words and then lose it in anger. But Romans 5 tells us that character comes through suffering and perseverance. God is building character into your children, through all the pain and difficulties in their lives—which may sometimes come from your hands.

You can't directly change the heart of your child. You can't even love them well for very long. You shall love the Lord your God. You shall also love your children well—because it is His love and will to love them, even through our mistakes.

The Love You Parent From

"O Love that will not let me go,
I rest my weary soul in Thee.
I give Thee back the life I owe,
That in Thine ocean's depths its flow
May richer, fuller be."
–George Mattheson

I met with three very fearful parents yesterday. We'll call them Jessica, Ellen, and Anne. Jessica came in to talk about her 14-year-old daughter. "She's making such good choices right now, but I get worried. And one thing I've noticed over the years, is that when I'm afraid is when I make mistakes as a mom." Ellen came in for an entirely different reason. "I'm afraid my children are never going to recover. I think I've lost myself and I'm scared . . . for them and for me." Anne was agitated. "I don't know what's going on with her. She should be helping me and be there for me, too, not just her friends. I'm just so disappointed in her."

Anne's daughter came in next. "I'm not sure what to do about my mom. I know she loves me, but sometimes I think she loves me too much."

So what does parenting out of love look like for these three? To Jessica, I want to say, you can have confidence in God's good for your daughter—that He loves her more than you could ever imagine and He has begun a good work in her that He will carry to completion. To Ellen, I want to say, be a person, not just a parent. Your children need to see you having life apart from them. And to Anne, your fear of losing your daughter is choking the life out of your relationship. She cannot be the center of your world. Seek life and love in the only One who can truly be in the center of our worlds and not disappoint us.

It's easy to think parenting out of love is parenting out of your own love. That you are supposed to love your children more—or better—or well. You can't. But you can parent out of a different kind of love. You can parent out of a love that won't let you go—or the child that you have entrusted to Him. And, as you lean into His love, you can parent out of love and not out of fear. You love because He first loved you. His love for you, as His child, just makes yours, for your child, that much richer and fuller.

The Greatest of These

"Now we see but a poor reflection as in a mirror; then we shall see face to face. Now I know in part; then I shall know fully, even as I am fully known. And now these three remain: faith, hope and love. But the greatest of these is love." –1 Corinthians 13:12-13, NIV

Every year at Christmas Eve, our family passed around the Bible and read the story of Jesus' birth. We would each read a line or two and pass it on to the next family member. Except my dad. He always passed the Bible on without reading it, which made sense. He was a quiet, unassuming man. He didn't like to draw attention to himself and didn't really even like to talk. One Christmas Eve, however, when the Bible came to him, he read. He didn't make a big deal out of it. No one said a word to him about it—or even to each other.

My dad had cancer at the time. I remember thinking, as he was reading, "Does he know something we don't know?" He died just a few short months later. I still think about him reading every Christmas Eve. I can see his face and hear his quiet voice. And, honestly, the one time he read impacted me more than all of the times he didn't.

For most of their growing up, your kids will be quick to point out your failures. But, in the end, love touches a deeper place. They remember the times you reached out, intentionally spending time with them. Or the times you laughed together, played games, or danced in the kitchen. They remember the way you believed in them and cheered them on. They remember the experience of relationship.

You may not hear from your children about how much you matter until your children have children of their own. In the long run, your son or daughter will remember. He will begin to see all the energy, time, hope, and love it took to raise him. She will finally begin to understand all of the hours and tears that poured into her growing up.

As you parent out of love, it is love that will reach deeper than your inevitable failure. They will remember and be grateful. And, honestly, they're grateful today—even if they're too young, or narcissistic, to admit it.

Who Do I Want to Be?

"You can be sure that God will take care of everything you need, his generosity exceeding even yours in the glory that pours from Jesus. Our God and Father abounds in glory that just pours out into eternity. Yes." –Philippians 4:19-20, The Message

I wonder how different my parenting would look if I managed to stop and consider what kind of person I want to be for my kids in the middle of some my personal messes. There are plenty as I survey my current existence. One mess is that my taxes are due in a couple of weeks, and can I just tell you that few things undo me quite like filing my taxes. It's strangely not even just about the money, it's the process. Accounting is to the therapist brain what nuclear engineering is to the artist brain. It looks like Greek to me. I stall, procrastinate, avoid, and deny my way to mid-April every year. I'm surprised my wife and kids don't move in with family or friends for the month.

I feel incompetent and clueless when it comes to filing my taxes. It's this moment that I have to reconcile myself to the truth that I'm not a great money manager. I have to evaluate how we spend as a family—sometimes wisely, sometimes not. I come face-to-face with how we measure up when it comes to stewardship. I also manage to question my vocational calling, how I don't provide enough for my family, how I compare myself to other men/providers, and all the junk that comes with that.

Filing taxes stirs me. And guess what I do? Eat. Chips and queso, chocolate chip cookies, cranberry pecan muffins, Ben and Jerry's, and on and on.

So my kids look around and see this anxious, irritable, over-extended, stress-induced, medicating-with-food father wandering about the house raiding the refrigerator and pantry. I don't think I'm communicating much about faith and hope in those weeks running up to my annual correspondence with Uncle Sam.

My kids need to see me wrestling with the big picture. They would strongly benefit from a father who set aside the panic, and chose to hand off all the anxiety, fear, shame, and insecurity to a God who longs to carry those things for me.

The Order of Things

"Love the Lord your God with all your heart and with all your soul and with all your strength. These commandments that I give you today are to be upon your hearts. Impress them on your children. Talk about them when you sit at home and when you walk along the road, when you lie down and when you get up. Tie them as symbols on your hands and bind them on your foreheads. Write them on the doorframes of your houses and on your gates." –Deuteronomy 6:5-9, NIV

Research tells us that children learn more from watching adults than from being told how to behave and feel. I don't know about you, but that data shakes me to the core. I often wonder what things my children have written in their journals about me over the years. I'd love to know and I'm terrified to know. I wonder about what mental notes they make about me as we move in and out of our days together. They have been and will continue to make lists of things they will and won't repeat in their own journey of parenting. Didn't we all make those lists?

I want to pay close attention to the order of the instruction in Deuteronomy. I think there is great parenting wisdom within that Scripture, especially sequence.

1. Love God with everything in me
2. Make sure the commandments are on my heart
3. Impress them on my children (live it out)
4. Talk about the commandments as we go along
5. Create reminders
6. Write them on the doorframes of my home

The order of things involves me doing a lot of work before I ever even open my mouth, and then again after I speak. In fact, out of those six instructions, only one of them involves talking about the commandments. Most of it involves loving God, assessing my heart, living a life a faith, creating reminders to love and making my home a place of love and worship. I'm instructed to speak only after I've loved God and assessed the state of my heart.

What great instruction for the daily rhythms of parenting. If I waited to discipline, to instruct, to teach, until I had connected with God and assessed myself, I'd likely interact differently with my kids.

The Run of the House

"God is love. When we take up permanent residence in a life of love, we live in God and God lives in us. This way, love has the run of the house, becomes at home and mature in us, so that we're free of worry on Judgment Day—our standing in the world is identical with Christ's. There is no room in love for fear. Well-formed love banishes fear." –1 John 4:16b-18a, The Message

Love banishes fear. Those are strong words. It's not that love intimidates fear, love convinces fear to leave, or even love fights fear. Love wins. Love not only wins, but sends fear from its very presence. Love banishes fear. God is love. There is no fear in Him.

God is not worried about your child. He doesn't wake up in the middle of the night wondering if she'll get in the right school or he'll make the team. He doesn't fear that your child will be hurt, make mistakes, or fail. He doesn't panic over if she'll find the right husband, if they'll have children or if he'll be successful.

He's not worried about your parenting, either. He doesn't fret over missed appointments or opportunities. He doesn't re-hash conversations, worried that the wrong thing was said or done. He doesn't worry that, because of your mistakes, your children will be "messed up forever."

God loves. He is love. When we take up permanent residence in a life of love, we live in God and God loves in us. And we, therefore, don't have to fear. His love has the power to banish our fear.

You will be stirred as a parent. The pain of your past will be stirred. The fear of the future—yours and theirs. You will be overwhelmed, at times, by who they are and all that they need. But love banishes fear. That love is where our hope comes from. And as we live in God, as we love Him and mature in him, we are able to entrust that which he has given to us back to him.

Give love the run of your homes—and your children. You and they will be glad you did.

A Day of Rest

"Oh! May the God of green hope fill you up with joy, fill you up with peace, so that your believing lives, filled with the life-giving energy of the Holy Spirit, will brim over with hope!" –Romans 15:13, The Message

We want you to take this day as a day of rest. Our prayer, today, is that you will find rest and refreshment through Christ. You are in the place He has chosen you to be. God is a God of hope, joy, and peace. May He grant you that today and this week in your journey to raising boys and girls.

Notes:

Additional Resources

The Explorer/Discovery Years

Books for You

Love and Logic Magic for Early Childhood, Jim Fay and Charles Fay
The Wonder of Boys, Michael Gurian
The Wonder of Girls, Michael Gurian
Becoming A Dad, Stephen James and David Thomas
Wild Things, Stephen James and David Thomas
Raising Girls, Melissa Trevathan and Sissy Goff

Authors We Love (for reading together)

Eric Carle
Kevin Henkes
Cynthia Rylant

Movies to Watch Together

Bedknobs and Broomsticks
Chitty Chitty Bang Bang
Peter Pan
The Lion King
Toy Story (1, 2, and 3)
Any of the *VeggieTales* series
Any of the Scholastic Books made into movies

The Lover/Adventurous Years

Books for You

Parenting with Love and Logic, Foster Cline and Jim Fay
Wild Things, Stephen James and David Thomas
Grace-Based Parenting, Tim Kimmel and Max Lucado
Raising Cain, Dan Kindlon and Michael Thompson
Parenting the Way God Parents, Katherine Koonce
Boys Should Be Boys, Meg Meeker
Sacred Parenting, Gary Thomas

Modern Parents, Vintage Values, Melissa Trevathan and Sissy Goff
Raising Girls, Melissa Trevathan and Sissy Goff
Queen Bees and Wannabees, Rosalind Wiseman
Stan and Brenna Jones's books about sex—four books that span a child's development

Books to Read Together
The *Anne of Green Gables* series, L.M. Montgomery
Little House on the Prairie series, Laura Ingalls Wilder
The American Girl historical books or character books
Secret Keeper Girl series, Dannah Gresh
Because of Winn-Dixie, Kate DiCamillo
Bridge to Terabithia, Katherine Paterson and Donna Diamond
The Percy Jackson series, Rick Riordan
The Little Prince, Antoine de Saint-Exupery
The Stories Julian Tells, Ann Cameron and Ann Strugnell
Stuart Little, E.B. White
The Wind in the Willows, Kenneth Grahame
The Complete Grimm's Fairy Tales, the Brothers Grimm

Movies to Watch Together
Any of the American Girl series
Babe
Because of Winn-Dixie
E.T.
It's a Wonderful Life
Mary Poppins
Miracle on 34th Street
Any of the Narnia series
The Sound of Music
The Wizard of Oz
Where the Red Fern Grows

The Individual/Narcissistic Years

Books for You

How Children Raise Parents, Dan Allender

Wild Things, Stephen James and David Thomas

Raising Girls, Melissa Trevathan and Sissy Goff

The Back Door to Your Teen's Heart, Melissa Trevathan and Sissy Goff

Modern Parents, Vintage Values, Melissa Trevathan and Sissy Goff

The 5 *Conversations* books, Vicki Courtney

Get Out of My Life, but First Could You Drive Me and Cheryl to the Mall, Anthony Wolf

Parenting Teens with Love and Logic, Foster Cline and Jim Fay

A Fine Young Man, Michael Gurian

(This is when the boys and girls start to separate from each other . . . and sometimes from you, although a couple of these books are designed to be read together.)

For Him

Flight Plan, Lee Burns and Braxton Brady (read together)

The Wilderking Trilogy, Jonathan Rogers

The Chronicles of Narnia series, C.S. Lewis

The Percy Jackson series, Rick Riordan

For Her

Mirrors and Maps, Melissa Trevathan and Sissy Goff (read together)

Between, Vicki Courtney

A Girl After God's Own Heart, Elizabeth George

Movies to Watch Together for Boys (although some girls like these, too)

Radio

Simon Birch

October Sky

Remember the Titans

Movies to Watch Together for Girls (and some boys might like these)
Freaky Friday
13 Going on 30—for the older girls
Nancy Drew
The Voyage of the Dawn Treader

The Wanderer/Autonomous Years

Books for You
Same as in previous list, but also:
The Best Old Movies for Families: A Guide to Watching Together, Ty
  Burr

Books for Him
How to Hit a Curve Ball, Stephen James and David Thomas
Do Hard Things, Alex Harris
Wild at Heart, John Eldredge

Books for Her
Growing Up Without Getting Lost, Melissa Trevathan and Sissy
  Goff
Teen Virtue, Vicki Courtney
Redeeming Love, Francine Rivers

Movies to Watch Together for Guys (although girls might like them, too)
Lord of the Rings series
My Dog Skip
The Outsiders
Finding Forrester

Movies to Watch Together for Girls
A Walk to Remember
Little Women
Pride and Prejudice
Emma

Answers for Listening Guides

Session 1

For young men, the risk of looking like a _fool_, the fear of being embarrassed, is so much stronger than the willingness to take the _risk_ to just be who God has _created_ them to be.

The girls were wondering, "Will I be left out? Will I just be left standing here?" Underneath, they just want to be _accepted_, to be _enjoyed_, to feel _safe_.

Underneath, the boys just want to have courage and _strength_. They want to be somebody. They just want to have some kind of _purpose_.

Madeleine L'Engle said that we are every _age_ we have ever _been_.

One dad said, "I wish I'd known how much _impact_ I had."

Failure is _inevitable_. But the important thing is that you stay _connected_.

You may recognize a _stage_ you feel stuck in.

Our desire is that you will be stirred to _love_.

We pray that you remember that God has _chosen_ you to be the parent of your child.

We want you to be convinced that God is able to _protect_ what you have _entrusted_ to Him.

Session 2

Relationship is foundational for girls across the age groups.

The first stage for girls is called the _Discovery_ _Years_ .

She is:
1. _Relational_
2. _Caretaking_
   Oxytocin is the _nurturing_ hormone.
3. _Imaginative_
   Imagination creates a fertile soil for _faith_ .
She needs:
1. _Boundaries_
   She needs structure, consequences, and _discipline_ ,
   because it helps her feel _safe_ .
2. _Freedom_
   There is a trend toward _anxiety_ in children.
3. _Delight_
   Girls who are delighted in feel more _delightful_ .

Boys in this stage are called _Explorers_ .

He is:
1. _Active_
   Boys tend to act first and then _think_ .
2. _Aggressive_
   Aggression is an expression of _intimacy_ .
3. _Curious_
He needs:
1. _Boundaries_
2. _Open_ _space_
   He needs an identified _space_ where he can take his
   anger or frustration.
3. _Consistency_

Session 3

Ages 6-10 for girls is the stage called the _Adventurous_
Years .

She is:
1. _Relational_
    Girls will develop a _relational_ strategy.
2. _Fearful_
    She needs very _literal_ answers to her _fear_ .
3. _Responsive_
She needs:
1. _Opportunity_
    A girl needs a "_north_ _star_," which is something she feels
    competent in.
2. _Unity_
    She needs you to present a _unified_ front.
3. _Grace_
    She needs you to become comfortable with the idea of
    failure .

Boys in this stage are called _Lovers_ .

He is:
1. _Tender_
    Ages 5-6 are known as the _kinder_ years.
2. _Obedient_
    He genuinely wants to _please_ .
3. _Competitive_
He needs:
1. _Reprieve_
    We best wake the male brain up by _movement_ .
2. _Routine_
    This is a good time to use _charts_ with boys.
3. _Regulation_
    Boys can become obsessively consumed with _media_ .

Session 4

This stage for girls is called the _Narcissistic_ _Years_.
She is:

1. _Relational_
    Relationships are what bring her the most _joy_ and the
    most _pain_.
2. _Insecure_
    The two things that her rapid brain development affects are
    her _memory_ and her _confidence_.
3. _Ambivalent_

She needs:

1. _Space_ to _grow_
    She needs _privacy_ and time to develop who she is.
2. _Strength_
    She needs you to be _stronger_ than she is.
3. A _back_ _door_
    To the degree that kids can _predict_ you, they will
    dismiss you.

Boys at this stage are called _Individuals_.
He is:

1. _Searching_
    Boys are primarily searching for _identity_ and
    masculinity.
2. _Evolving_
3. _Experimenting_
    He is experimenting with _profanity_ and _breaking_ the
    rules. Boys crave _power_ and _purpose_.

He needs:

1. _Involvement_
2. _Information_
3. _Outlets_
    He needs outlets to test his _strength_, test
    his _mind_, feel _risk_ and adventure,
    and feel _purpose_.

RAISING BOYS AND GIRLS

Session 5

Stage 4 for girls is called the _Autonomous_ _Years_.

She is:

1. _Relational_

    These are the years when _sex_ becomes much more of an issue.

2. _Post-pubescent_

    As girls get older, they get _curvier_.

    Eating disorders are about two things: _self-hatred_ and _control_.

3. _Her_ _own_ _person_

    We want them to have _voices_.

She needs:

1. _Respect_

2. _Room_ to _grow_

    You want to _widen_ the _parameters_ incrementally.

3. _Wings_

A boy at this stage is called the _Wanderer_.

He is:

1. _In_ _biological_ _chaos_

    He is experiencing between 5-7 extra surges of _testosterone_ a day.

2. _Arrogant_ and _argumentative_

    His arrogance is a cover for his _insecurity_.

3. _Individuating_

He needs:

1. _Other_ _voices_

2. _Mercy_

3. _Limitations_

    He is an experiential _learner_.

You need a parenting _community_.

Session 6

With _naming_, you are _calling_ out who God has _made_ your _child_ to be.

Ingredients of naming:
1. _Enjoyment_—Enjoyment of who _we_ are and who _they_ are
2. _Dealing_ with your own _stuff_
3. _Celebrating_—We celebrate them when they _succeed_ and when they _fail_

You cannot directly _change_ the _heart_ of a child.

The quality of _relationship_ is what lasts.

There is a healthy _fear_ and _awareness_ of what's going on.

But the fear can begin to _paralyze_ us.

Confidence comes from a combination of _hope_ and _trust_.

Parent out of _love_ and not out of _fear_.

Parenting out of love is being willing to _humble_ yourself.

Don't lose _heart_.

God's perfect _love_ casts out _fear_.

RAISING BOYS AND GIRLS